Dedicated in loving memory to my
Auntie Joyce Cartwright.

Thank you
I Miss You.

FOR CRYING out loud

CHERYL FRAMPTON

HARTSMERE

Some of the names in this book have been changed
to protect their identity.

HARTSMERE Publishers
Tamarack House
44 Newport Road
Saffron Walden
CB11 4BS.
Email hartsmere@msn.com

The Author asserts the moral right to be
identified as the author of this work

ISBN 0-9543234-0-8

Cover Design by
Mark Smith Typographics, Horley
Surrey. RH6 0AG

Typeset and Printed in Great Britain by
Printwise (Haverhill) Limited, Suffolk

Written with Leigh Ferrani

Acknowledgements

I am eternally grateful to my wonderful husband Nigel, whose love and belief in me has never faltered. There are not enough words to express my love and respect; you are my hero. You have an awesome spirit that truly inspires me and my love for you will remain forever.

Thanks to my sons Shane and Lee - my greatest achievements in life. Shane, you have given me such joy and happiness and I'm so proud of who you have become and what you have already achieved. Lee, your love and sense of humour still amazes and fills me with laughter. You have both shown great courage over the years. The two of you have so much to offer and I cannot express deeply enough the enduring love I have for you.

To my sisters: you are brave women and have been behind me wholeheartedly in the writing of this book. I know it hasn't been an easy ride for you and we have indeed come full circle. I love you both. Thank you so much.

Dad, I want you to know I'm grateful for your love and loyalty during the most difficult times. You were my lifeline and nothing can compare with that. You saved my soul on many occasions, without realising. I'm proud, and will always be proud, to be your daughter.

Uncle Victor, Uncle Stan, Auntie Peggy and Uncle Bert, who is sadly no longer with us, despite the grief I brought you, you all gave your love and constant support, even when I knew I didn't deserve it. Not once did you let me down and I'll never be able to thank you enough. Please know that I'm eternally grateful and love you all dearly.

Jill and Robin, you are the best sister-in-law and brother-in-law anyone could ask for. Thank you for your encouragement and advice whenever I needed it. Hugs and kisses.

If it weren't for you, Mike Linnett, I'd never have seen Shane grow up. You gave me faith in social workers and I know that you laid your career and reputation on the line for me. Without your belief in me as a person and mother I'd never have managed to win custody of Shane. You always play this down, but you won't get away with it this time. You changed our lives. May God bless you, Mike. Thank you.

Mum, I wouldn't be the person I am without the experiences we have shared. I know things have broken down between us and, regrettably, we can probably never have a proper mother and daughter relationship, but I bear you no malice or bad feeling. We all have our own path to walk in this life. We can only do our best and I hope that you find the happiness you are searching for.

This book would never have been printed if it weren't for my friend and publisher, Cliff Treadwell. You believed in this story and understood my intention to try to help others. Not for one moment have I underestimated the risk you've taken. I only hope that now, despite the drama of it all, we're there, and onto the next. Thank you so, so much.

If ever I've driven anyone insane it was Leigh Ferrani, my

editor, writer and friend. You understood what I was trying to say despite the unusual way I have of expressing myself. You found my voice and kept the spirit alive. You are one talented, crazy mate and thank you just doesn't seem enough.

Another big thank you goes to Helen Corner at Cornerstones, whose editorial service has been a tremendous help to me.

There have been many people who have been instrumental in my life. It would take another chapter just to list them all, but there have been many friends who have stuck by me over the years, even with all my dramas landing at their door. Jennie Holben, Suzie Pavlovic, Jean Elliott and Suzie Hardimon: I have been privileged to know you and I'm grateful for all you've done. I know that no matter what, we are all there for each other and I'm truly blessed to have friends as dear as you. Ian, Amanda, Ann, Phil, Charlie and Pockets the dog, you are great mates and have been there for Nigel and me more than you've realised. Thank you.

Last, but not least, thanks to Jo and Chris Frampton. Believe me when I tell you both that despite our ups and downs over the years, I'm proud of who you are and what you've achieved for yourselves. You've taught me so much and I hope I've been able to give something back to you. Much love.

Foreword

People who don't know me might ask why I have written this book. I'm not famous; I've never been featured on the news, I'm relieved to say; and I haven't come up with a cure for cancer or patented a life-changing invention that's been marketed worldwide. What I have done is lived through a life that has challenged and tested me, to the extent where I sometimes thought I might not come through it; that I may not survive. These doubts never took root, or stayed in my head for very long because I always knew that with the hope and belief that there is so much more to human life than what we can see, what we can touch, taste, buy or own, I would get through the hard times.

I have written this book simply to pass on this message, so that others who have suffered violence, difficult family relationships and experiences similar or dissimilar to mine may be comforted in the knowledge that nothing is permanent and no situation lasts forever. With a positive faith in ourselves and the ability to see the funny side, we can remember that we are here to experience, learn and find our own place in the world. With this insight follows a greater sense of peace, regardless of what's thrown in our way.

People I've met throughout my life have asked me how I coped with the suicide of my first husband and how I survived years of physical and mental abuse. All I can say is that from a very young age I've always known I'm not alone. Even as a small girl I knew that whatever happened to me I would be all right, and I continue to believe that there is an unseen hand, or hands, guiding me. I am absolutely positive in my conviction that there's something beyond our physical world.

I have asked myself over and over whether I should publish my story. I have fretted over the fact that those close to me will be affected and that others might accuse me of seeking monetary gain or retribution. But filling my pockets has never been a driving force in my life, and revenge is for those driven by anger or fear. With the continuing encouragement of my dear sons and husband, and my sisters and friends, I finally laid my doubts to rest and stopped questioning myself. I now know that putting my story to paper is the right thing to do.

For Crying Out Loud takes my loved ones and me to the end of one road and onto a positive and happy place. I sincerely hope that anyone reading this book has found or will soon find that place too.

Chapter One

In 1968 my mum and dad announced that we were moving from Mitcham in Surrey to Australia. I was eleven years old and not at all happy about leaving my friends and school. My oldest sister, Lucy, and her husband Robert had chosen to come with us, but my other sister, Sheena, wanted to stay in England because she was settled here.

Some people might have considered me spoilt. Because I was so much younger than my sisters, my mum would buy me flash clothes in the latest fashions and I enjoyed getting dressed up as most young girls do. But while I never went without, I yearned for Mum's approval and the certainty that she loved me. I think she did, but she never voiced it and wasn't able to open up and show affection for another person – particularly those related to her.

A social butterfly and the wittiest person in the room at parties, but Mum was distant with her family and could stop us in our tracks with one stern look from her piercing brown eyes. She was tall and possessed a forbidding character; someone you didn't dare cross for fear of the consequences.

I always thought Mum looked Spanish and I picked up on the fact that she had the kind of looks that turned heads when she walked into a room. Men would almost break their necks in an attempt to get a better view of my mother.

Dad was a big, kind man, with a gentle disposition and a love of the simple things in life. He owned several butcher shops that seemed to be thriving, thanks to his hard work and the long hours he put in. I wouldn't say we were that well off, but we were comfortable and went on holidays abroad at least once a year.

Next to one of my dad's butcher shops was a hairdressing salon. I used to love going in there and sweeping up all the hair on the floor into piles. The owner of the salon was a lady with bright red hair called Carol, who would give me sixpence if I did a good job, and I'd immediately run to the sweetshop.

Carol's boyfriend Gordon would sit me on his knee and tell me all sorts of stories. He soon became Uncle Gordon to me. Little did I know that he was about to be famous.

One day a refrigerator, tied up in a red bow was delivered to my father's shop.

'Go and get Lucy love,' Dad said.

I ran upstairs to fetch my sister. 'Quick Lucy, a big present just arrived for you.'

Lucy looked surprised and ran downstairs. She could hardly contain herself.

'Who's it from, who's it from?' I screamed.

Trembling, she read the card. 'Congratulations on your wedding. You owe me one. Love Gordon.'

He never did get to Lucy's wedding and I never got to sit on his lap again and listen to his stories because he was arrested for his part in the Great Train Robbery. His full name was Gordon Goody and he was the topic of conversation in my parent's household for sometime to come. But eventually things settled down once again.

Even as a child, I thought that my parents had nothing in common and couldn't work out how on earth two such different personalities had managed to end up together.

Mum was a glamour queen and Dad had a round belly, big hands and feet that looked liked two great big boats stuck on the end of his legs. My nickname for my father was Billy Bunter.

Perhaps after going through a nervous breakdown as a result of physical abuse at the hands of her first husband, the father of my two sisters, Mum was searching for a secure relationship and saw Dad as safe and steadfast; her escape route.

My dad came into my mother's life at the right time. She'd been discharged from hospital and Lucy and Sheena were living in a children's home until she recovered from her breakdown.

Mum and my sisters tell different versions of this story, but it's not fair for me to comment because I wasn't born then. My sisters agree that although any kind of physical violence is totally unacceptable, both Mum and their dad were unfaithful and both were verbally, and physically abusive to one another.

Sheena in particular felt abandoned and unloved by Mum and still, decades later, cannot and will not forgive Mum for all the hurt she has caused Sheena and those around her.

After finding out she was pregnant with her second child, Mum was hoping to have a boy and was disappointed when Sheena was born. Her distaste was so strong that, as a tiny newborn, Sheena was thrown onto the bed and called 'a fucking black-eyed bastard.' Mum often repeated the insult during the years that followed. Sheena was dark like Mum, not light-haired and blue-eyed like Lucy and me, and her disappointment at not giving birth to a male child eventually reached a peak when she accused Sheena of breaking up her marriage because 'she didn't have a handle,' a penis in less crude terms.

When I was little I spent a lot of time sitting on my dad's knee listening to him talk of the night he met my mother. He said he was blown away by her beauty and vivacious manner, and fell in love with her as soon as he set eyes on her in a smoky pub.

Sadly, it was plain that Mum never felt the same passion for Dad. He wasn't interested in parties and smart clothes; he lived in his tatty green cardigan with big brown buttons that I'd fiddle with when I was small, and he also adored his comfy shoes, which he never laced up, so you could hear him scuffling from a mile away. Mum often scolded him, snapping 'Do your bloody shoes up,' but they always managed to come undone again.

I've often wondered if Mum only agreed to have me because Dad wanted a child of his own. She'd already given birth to two girls, who were ten and twelve years older than me, and she fancied more fun and adventure - the kind of existence that didn't centre on bringing up kids. I suspect that the reason we went to Australia was because Mum was desperate to live a glamorous lifestyle in the sun, and that was probably the real reason why there was one extra emigrant joining us on the ship to Oz.

For months prior to our leaving England, it turned out that Mum had been having an affair with a twenty-one-year-old neighbour, The Lad. That's exactly how I referred to him: not to his face, of course because Mum would have clipped me around the ear for being rude.

At the time Mum was forty-one, and although I was very young and knew nothing of sex and adult relationships, I wondered why The Lad was always in our house.

Their first meeting was an occasion that brought heartache for me and I never forgot that day as I grew up. One afternoon, Mum asked The Lad, who worked for the RSPCA, to come over and catch my pet rat Willy, who'd escaped from our garden shed, where I kept an army of small, fluffy animals. I adored animals and spent hours talking to them. I think because my sisters were so much older than me I felt like an only child, so my pets were my playmates and Willy was one of my favourites.

Unbelievably, The Lad caught Willy and then drowned him in a bucket of water. My mother had sent me to my room, so I didn't know what had actually happened until afterwards, but I can still hear my beloved pet's terrified squeals as he was suffocated.

Mum said she had agreed that The Lad should kill Willy because she reckoned domesticated rats turned wild when they escaped and could be infected with a disease fatal to humans if bitten. I think she just didn't want Willy around because he was 'vermin.' I cried and cried for days and from then on I hated that bloody lad. Meanwhile, he and Mum grew closer and closer.

The day I realised there was more to their relationship than friendship happened to be the day I had my first sex education lesson at school. I dashed home from school, desperate to tell Mum that I'd seen a picture of a penis. I remember the stifled snorts that echoed around the classroom as a diagram of what I called 'a sausage and two sprouts' was held up for the scrutiny of thirty kids.

Rushing into the lounge, I was horrified to find Mum kissing and cuddling The Lad, who was now lodging with us, on the sofa. As I ran out into the kitchen, where Lucy was, Mum followed me.

'Why were you kissing him, Mummy?' I sobbed.

Mum tried to reassure me that nothing was going on, that that they had been doing the crossword together. Now I might have been young, but daft, I wasn't, and I was pretty sure that was the most unusual way of doing the crossword I'd ever seen.

I decided it was time to leave home. I packed a chocolate bar and an apple in my lunchbox and yelled 'I'm running away now!' giving the front door a good slam for dramatic effect. I had no money on me, so I don't know where I thought I was going. I only got as far as the end of the street before The Lad caught up with me and pulled me to a stop with a yank on my long hair.

'Why don't you leave my Mummy alone? I'm telling my daddy on you!' I shouted on the way back to the house.

Feeling very scared of this young man I rang my dad at work and told him I'd had an argument with Mum and The Lad. Of course, I didn't want to hurt Dad by telling him what I'd witnessed in his own home because I dearly loved my father and didn't want my parents to split.

Dad was furious and reassured me that he'd come home and sort everything out. How relieved I was when I heard the familiar shuffle of his huge shoes on the front path.

As Dad entered the house, The Lad came out of the kitchen, probably intending to slink off somewhere, but I was glad to see Dad push him back inside before instructing me to leave the room.

I had a strong suspicion that Dad was sure something was going on between Mum and our lodger because he'd been quieter than usual and had taken to sitting fiddling with a matchbox, turning it over and over in his hands, lost in his own world and probably wondering what to do to about his marriage. I felt like crying to see him so downhearted and unlike his usual cheerful self, and I wanted to shake my mother for what she was doing to him.

I think the argument I'd had with Mum and The Lad was the last straw and an argument broke out. I couldn't hear exactly what was said, but loud voices filled the house, making me feel scared and alone.

The argument made me think back to one evening months before. I was watching TV and my parents and sisters were in the kitchen, when I overheard Dad asking Mum whether she was having an affair with The Lad. Mum denied it and Lucy backed her story up, probably having been warned not to say anything. My mother was extremely good at emotional blackmail and I know Lucy wouldn't have found the courage to go against Mum's wishes. It wasn't long before I found out exactly why Lucy often sided with Mum.

Sheena was always one to speak her mind though, and refused to be cowed by Mum. However much Mum insulted, bashed or bullied Sheena, she wouldn't cry, wouldn't say 'sorry' for any so-called slip-up and wouldn't give Mum the satisfaction of winning one over on her. Sheena wasn't prepared to lie to Dad's face either, and a terrible row continued. I couldn't bear to hear any more, so I put my fingers in my ears and ran to my room in tears.

It was just after this episode that my parents announced that we were going to Australia to start a new life. I really wasn't happy about this decision, partly because I'd just started to do some modeling, which I was absolutely thrilled about. I would sit in my room picturing myself sashaying down a catwalk in designer gear, camera bulbs flashing and people applauding. I wanted to be the next Twiggy, not spend a month on a ship, which was going to dock in some strange land on the other side of the world. I was resentful towards my parents and sulked often, but it did nothing to change Mum and Dad's minds and during the following couple of months they planned the big move.

As I said in the foreword to this book, from a very young age I have felt that there was someone looking out for me, guiding me, and it was during this period of upheaval that something truly extraordinary happened.

As Mum and Dad busied themselves with travel preparations I began to hear the sound of bells ringing. They reminded me of old-fashioned school bells – the sort of ones that teachers would ring to signal the end of playtime. With my heart pounding, I plucked up the courage to find out where the ringing sound was coming from and was led to my parents' bedroom. I took a deep breath and slowly opened the door to the room, where the bells suddenly stopped. For some reason my initial fear completely dissolved and I felt a strong urge to laugh. I had a damn good chuckle in fact, finding the whole thing odd but comical.

I'd had strange experiences before but had never dared tell anyone, knowing that no adult would take me seriously, putting it down to a child's fertile imagination working overtime.

The ringing of the bells went on for several days and I doubted anyone other than me had noticed them, until I heard my mum and dad talking in the kitchen. Mum was telling Dad she could hear a ringing sound and it was scaring her. I was surprised that I wasn't the only one hearing this strange noise, but I was even more surprised at Mum admitting to being frightened. I had thought my mother was untouchable, collected and in control at all times.

Dad laughed, saying it was the bell on the collar of the teddy bear belonging to their granddaughter Leanne. However, the bells continued and eventually my dad and The Lad heard them too. I found the whole situation terribly exciting and told my friends what was going on. They probably thought I'd lost the plot.

Mum didn't find the bells remotely funny, so she made us all swap our bedrooms, thinking this would somehow rid the house of our invisible bell ringer, but the noise continued to dog her wherever she slept.

At her wits' end, my mother decided to go to a medium in the hope that she'd find out what was going on. I had no idea what a medium did, so Mum explained everything to me - and the fact that the medium had told her that the ringing sound was coming from her spirit guide, a monk who was trying to contact her. The medium advised my mum to acknowledge the guide's presence and promised the noise would then stop.

For a while the ringing did cease, but it returned when we were on the ship to Perth. I was glad because I had missed them when they were gone. I liked and was comforted by the fact that we had a monk emigrating with us, and couldn't understand why the others were so upset. Soon he became my invisible friend and I'd chatter away to him, but after a while the bells disappeared. Perhaps the monk had got bored with me rattling on about how homesick I was.

To this day, I still can't work out why The Lad came with us to Australia. The only reason I can come up with as to why my father didn't send him packing was because he was afraid my mother would leave him and run off with The Lad. You see, Dad loved my mum so much he would have done anything for her – even to the detriment of his own pride and happiness. I guessed he was hoping their affair would run its natural course and fizzle out. However, inviting The Lad along with us was more than I could understand or accept, and I know my sisters were dismayed by the situation as well. They'd built up a good relationship with my father, who treated them like his own daughters.

The day of our departure was a sad one - not just because we were leaving our friends and home behind but Sheena wasn't coming with us. The relationship between her and Mum had become more of a strain on both of them, so it was probably for the best. Sheena was happy to remain behind in England.

The day we embarked I was upset, but excited too. I thought what a big adventure it all was and clutched my doll to my chest, waving goodbye to our family and friends on the dockside.

We set sail with the ship's horn blowing loudly and went to begin a brand new life, along with hundreds of others hoping for a brighter future in Australia.

Chapter Two

The name of our ship was Fairstar. It was two stories high and had everything you'd need for a comfortable journey - a hairdresser's, a cinema, shops, restaurants and bars. I had a wonderful time during our voyage and made loads of friends my own age; I even met my first boyfriend. He was called Shane and was blond and handsome; so I decided that if I had a son I'd name him Shane too.

When I wasn't with Shane or my other friends I'd spend as much time as I could with my dad. Only he still wasn't his usual chirpy self and appeared lonely and depressed to me. I wished I could help him or say something to make him feel better, but I was a child and didn't have the right words to soothe his pain. All I could do was be with him and try my best to take his mind off his worries. I'd spend hours listening to him as he told me about his exciting days in the Navy. We'd enjoy afternoons strolling around the huge deck or playing cards. I sensed that he knew I was trying to be a comfort to him and I think he was grateful for my company. This period brought us even closer together than before.

It was during the voyage that I again realised that my sense of fear wasn't nearly as strong as other people's and that my knowledge that I'd be safe and looked after was always with me. There were times when the weather was rough and I saw that many of the passengers, both adults and children, were shaken and cried out in fear, but I couldn't understand why they were so distressed. Don't ask me how, but I was positive there was nothing to worry about and I wished I could tell people this. I knew no one would listen though. They'd have thought I was daft.

On several occasions, the passengers were ushered in life jackets into the main hall by the crew, until the weather changed and the waves were gentle once more. I found it quite funny seeing all the tables and chairs slide back and forth from one end of the hall to another, and all the adults trying to hang onto them, while some of us kids played a game of hit and miss with them.

The storm reminded me of an incident that had happened not long before we set off for Australia. We were on holiday in Spain and I was playing with my bucket and spade on a sand bank in the sea. I'd forgotten to put my inflatable arm bands on and, out of nowhere, a freak tidal wave rose up and washed me right out to sea. I was under the water, unable to breathe, but I wasn't scared; I didn't even kick or struggle. I just floated about under the water and felt completely calm, and then suddenly I was plucked from the sea, placed on the sand and given mouth-to-mouth resuscitation, until the water left my air passage and I could breathe freely again.

I was told afterwards that the man who'd saved me was a swimming teacher, but I didn't get the chance to thank him because I never saw him again.

My mum was furious that I'd almost drowned and blamed the rest of the family for not keeping a closer eye on me. I couldn't understand what all the fuss was about, as the whole experience had been quite unreal: enjoyable in a weird way. I remember thinking that if death was like that then I had nothing to be scared of. I don't have a fear of death to this day.

After a month at sea we docked in Fremantle, Perth, and were taken to a hostel for British immigrants. I opened the trunk that was packed with my Barbie dolls, precious books and other belongings and was annoyed to find that everything was ruined by mildew and smelled musty. My dolls and favourite items were all I had left of my past life and now I had to throw them away. I kicked one of my Barbies across the room and slumped on the edge of my bed. 'I want to go home,' I blubbed. 'I want to go home!'

Thankfully, we weren't in the immigrant hostel long because I hated the place – especially meal times, where we ate tasteless food on long trestle tables that put me in mind of the times I'd visited Butlin's with my parents. As there were so many residents our breakfast and dinner was served in several sittings. By the time we got our food it was invariably cold. I imagined what it must have been like to be in the Army, lining up for lumpy mashed potato and gravy.

I knew Mum and my sister didn't like their surroundings, which wasn't surprising, considering that everyone was crammed into rows and rows of tiny shed-like tin huts with corrugated roofs that made creaking noises at night. It was a blessed relief for everyone when we moved into a maisonette in a pretty part of Perth, and Lucy and Robert found a place nearby.

I found life in Australia strange at first and often missed England and my old friends. The heat was often unbearable, but eventually I settled in to school and was very popular because of my unusual accent and trendy clothes, which were miles ahead of Perth in the style stakes.

Although I was settling down, I wasn't pleased that I was having to share a room with The Lad. Our house only had two bedrooms, so my parents were occupying the main bedroom and our 'lodger' and I the other. At the time I didn't know that such a situation was inappropriate; I just didn't like this young man because he spent too much time with my mum.

It's more than likely that Mum would much rather have been sharing a double bed with her attractive young lover than my trusty dad. Dad was probably painfully aware of this fact, but being a soft man went along with the charade to keep up appearances and hide the truth from me. He carried on pretending that The Lad was a paying guest and no more.

Mum wanted me to see The Lad as a brother and treat him as such, but I wasn't having any of it. 'You're a big pain in the bum, you are,' I often told him when Mum was out of earshot.

So it appeared that Dad had sold his businesses and moved to the opposite side of the world with his family, only to share his own home with some kid who was having sex with the woman he loved – practically under his nose. When I think of the situation now it seems shocking. I'm just glad I was so young and wasn't entirely sure what was going on.

But events were to become even more bizarre. My parents left our cosy maisonette and bought a small caravan in which to travel around Australia. The Lad and I were in bunk beds at one side of the van and Mum and Dad slept in a foldout bed on the other, which doubled as our kitchen table. How The Lad felt about seeing Mum in bed with another man I've no idea, because nothing was said and an atmosphere of friendliness was kept at all times. Dad must have been a saint because he was nice to The Lad. Don't ask me how on earth he kept his temper in check. Personally, I think even the mildest man, finding himself in my dad's place, would have landed the swine a well-earned smack on the nose and kicked his wife out for her cheek.

When I talk with Dad now he admits to feeling 'very stupid for letting them get away with it.' Still, it's so very easy to regret your actions when looking back over time and events. My Dad hadn't committed a crime; he just fell for the wrong person.

Not only did I have to share a caravan with The Lad: because we were on the move so much I couldn't stay in one school, so he was given the job of teaching me.

It was the law back then that any child who couldn't attend lessons on a continuous basis had to be taught by correspondence and it was also stipulated that no family member could take the role of teacher. We were travelling through such a remote part of Australia that we couldn't find anyone who could teach me by correspondence regularly, so that's why The Lad had to do it.

I wasn't impressed with this plan at all and made sure I was as difficult as possible by not listening to a single word he said. I don't think he was unintelligent, but I didn't want him to assume I found his teaching remotely interesting and I made this plain by looking as bored as I could. I'd stare out of the window, yawn loudly and stretch my arms above my head. My attitude infuriated The Lad and eventually he gave up.

'Hah,' I thought, 'serves you right, you little shit.'

We carried on travelling across the Nullarbor with its dry and dusty roads that covered the car and van in a thick red mist. You could see the heat rising from the ground, and we had to have big, metal 'roo bars fixed to the front of the car because the kangaroos would hop out in front of you with no warning.

The outback stretched out before us, and I'd get restless with nothing to occupy my mind, so I'd continuously sing 'Blanket on the Ground', which was a popular song then.

'Stop that bloody singing, Cheryl,' Mum would bark.

It became painfully tedious; the four of us cramped in a sweatbox on wheels and we spent hours playing a game called Frustration. It was a round plastic contraption filled with dice that made a popping sound as it was rolled about. That sound got on our nerves so much that I think Mum was tempted to hurl the game out of the window on many occasions, except we had no other form of entertainment. Frustration was the perfect name for that game and even now I can't bear the sight of it or sound of it.

I was dying to live a normal home life, especially as Christmas was on its way and I was worried as to how we were going to fit a tree in the caravan.

We travelled through many towns and cities until we reached Adelaide, which my father loved at once and called 'The City of Lights' because of the lovely night views with the stars and streetlights twinkling in the distance. My father decided he liked the place so much he'd buy a maisonette there. I couldn't believe the size of it and thought we were living in a mansion.

Having spent all his savings on our new home, Dad couldn't afford to give his family a lavish Christmas that year, so I didn't receive my usual pillowcase full of gifts. Instead, when out shopping with my father in Woolworth's, I pointed at pads and pens, saying that was what I wanted for Christmas - not a bike or new clothes. It also dawned on me that because I had to pick out my own presents that Santa didn't exist, which meant I didn't press my nose against the window on Christmas Eve, looking for Rudolph and the other reindeers.

Christmas morning came and I peeled off the paper wrapped around my presents.

'Ooh, that's lovely. Thanks, Daddy,' I said, and then, 'Thank you, Mum.' I kissed both my parents on the cheek, pretending to be surprised. I felt in some way that it was my fault that Mum and Dad weren't very well off and I didn't want them to think I was ungrateful for what they had given me.

The Lad had splashed out on a gift for me. He handed me a brightly wrapped parcel, which I opened to find a blue nylon suit that was made up of a pleated skirt with a thick elasticated waist and matching top that was fastened with a chunky zip. I'm sure he'd gone around the shops in search of the most ugly outfit he could find and one that would make me as uncomfortable as possible in the scorching weather. He looked at me expectantly and I mumbled a word of thanks, egged on by Mum, who was obviously thinking that her bit on the side and her child were doing some Yuletide bonding.

Mum, however, thought it was the most beautiful outfit she'd ever set eyes on and made me sweat in it all day. The Lad could have gift-wrapped a pound of pork sausages for me and she would have fallen over with delight.

We were in the middle of a long heat wave and I was sleeping in the bath to stay cool when I overheard my parents having a row. Mum was saying that she wanted to fly to Perth to help Lucy with her second child, Rebecca, with whom she was having problems. Dad reminded Mum that money was tight and it wasn't a good time for her to be shelling out on plane tickets. Mum shocked me by blurting that she had to go because 'Rebecca isn't Robert's, but John's.'

Not being able to take in what I'd heard I clambered out of the bath and tiptoed to the door, placing an eager ear against the wood. Mum went on to explain that Lucy had had an affair with a good mutual friend of the couple's and the result of this relationship was Rebecca. Dad's surprise showed in his voice: he obviously knew nothing about this.

'I can't believe it,' I muttered, 'It can't be true. Not Lucy.'

It turned out that Rebecca was having behavioural problems and wasn't as quick to learn as her sister, Leanne, and Lucy was experiencing feelings of wanting to harm her baby.

Mum said she was worried that my sister might do something silly and pointed out that Lucy couldn't turn to her husband for support because he knew nothing of the affair.

Days later Mum flew to Perth, leaving me with Dad. I was pleased because it meant I could be on my own with my father and it also gave me an opportunity to aggravate The Lad as much as possible. I did wonder if I should tell either one of my parents I 'd overheard them talking about Lucy's secret, but thought it better to keep my mouth shut. It was adult business after all – plus I didn't fancy being told off by Mum for being 'a nosy sod.'

Mum returned after a few weeks, which was a great relief for The Lad because I had to go back to being polite. Then, once more, my parents announced that we were moving.

Our new house was even better than our last one and in a prettier area. I had a huge room all to myself, Mum and Dad were still sharing a room – although they slept in separate beds by now - and The Lad had the room next to mine. Both my parents found work, Dad as a butcher and Mum as a nurse, but I can't remember what The Lad did for a living at that point. Probably very little, knowing him.

I started a new school and tried to make friends, but this time it was difficult for me because I was so far behind with my schoolwork and felt as if I was a failure. I was fourteen and decided the best course of action to take was to become a pop star. This I have to blame partly on my David Cassidy obsession.

Things seemed to be looking up when Sheena, her husband Adam and her family came to Australia to live, but the same old problems didn't disappear just because we were all in a country thousands of miles from Britain, and soon Mum and Sheena had begun to clash worse than before. One day I got home from school to find Mum standing by the side of the road crying hysterically. She didn't appear to realise what she was doing or where she was. All I managed to get out of her was that she'd had another row with Sheena. I was scared, as I'd never seen my mother lose control, so I ran to the phone and called Dad.

'Dad, Mum's going nuts. She's fallen out with Sheena again. Can you come home and sort her out?' I asked, tears running down my face.

My father reassured me he was on his way and eventually he managed to calm Mum down. What that argument was about, I'll never know, but it was obvious that their relationship was irreparable.

It seemed events were going to take another unfortunate turn, but not for my mother - for The Lad. One day Mum and The Lad decided to take my friend and me to the National Park. While we were there Mum handed me her instant Polaroid camera and asked me to take a shot of her and The Lad together. Reluctantly, I pointed the camera at them and took the picture. The four of us waited for the photo to develop and were amazed to see what looked exactly like a monkey squatting on The Lad's head. Everyone apart from The Lad fell about laughing and couldn't work out how such a thing had happened. We were standing in a section of the park where there were no animals at all – let alone a large, brown chimpanzee. Mum managed to calm The Lad down by promising to get the camera and film checked out.

The Lad was even more annoyed when I spent the rest of the day scratching my head and making chimp noises. He was fuming when we went to a café to get something to eat and I asked 'fancy a banana split with your coffee?' I think it occurred to me then that The Lad didn't have the strongest sense of humour I'd ever come across, but that just made me laugh at him all the more.

After the park we went to the cinema to watch, ironically, 'Love Story' and then headed home. But The Lad's day was far from over. When we got back to the house I made tea for everyone and when I passed The Lad his cup he jumped out of his seat.

'What kind of game are you playing?' he yelled. I thought he'd flipped, until he showed Mum and me the contents of his cup. It was filled to the brim with black, liquid shoe polish. Mum knew I couldn't have done it; we didn't have liquid shoe polish in the house and we never had. We were flabbergasted.

'Bloody kid!' said The Lad and stomped off to his room.

Moments later he came flying back into the kitchen, threatening me with all sorts. He'd found his alarm clock balanced on his curtain pole and thought I was the perpetrator. How on earth he thought I could have managed such a feat without the use of a ladder I had no idea and I burst out laughing again.

'Stop fucking laughing,' warned Mum, 'or you'll get a clout.'

My mum took the camera to be checked for faults, but no one found anything wrong with it, so Mum decided to get a medium to visit our house. The medium took one glance at me and said it was I who was encouraging the disruptive presence of a poltergeist. She also told Mum that I was psychic and to prove it gave me the ring of someone who she knew, but I didn't. The lady asked me to tell her what kind of person owned the piece of jewellery and what that person looked like. I thought she was a bit mad, so I simply said what came into my head: that the owner of the ring was an older lady of short stature, who suffered with a breathing condition and had a bad temper but liked to laugh at herself a lot. She also wore funny stockings. The medium told us that the ring had belonged to her mother, who fitted my description perfectly; the breathing condition was asthma and the funny stockings were support stockings. I went on to inform the medium that her mother had been loving towards her and that she wanted her daughter to carry on with her work as a medium.

We were amazed at the accuracy of my description and the medium was enthusiastic for me to develop my gift as she had, but Mum wasn't keen on me getting involved with something she knew little about – especially at my age. I was glad because I was much more interested in teenage pastimes like hanging out with my friends and listening to my David Cassidy records.

Chapter Three

It was a few weeks after my sixteenth birthday when my parents sat me down at the kitchen table and gave me the news I'd always dreaded: that they were separating. I'd been told by Mum countless times before that she was stuck with Dad because of me, but I'd ignored the truth, persuading myself that my parents loved each other and they would stay together forever.

In reality, my mum was desperate to leave my father and wanted to set up home with her lover now that I was 'grown up' and old enough to cope with it. Dad said he was going to share a house with a male acquaintance who was also divorced and that there was no spare room for me. It wasn't far from where we were living at the time, but I hated the thought of not seeing him every day and wanted to live with him.

My resentment towards The Lad was worse than ever and it was clear that he was less than enthusiastic where I was concerned. He knew he had greater influence over Mum than anyone in the family and constantly reminded me how Mum loved him more than her other children and me. Although I denied this to his face I believed that what he was saying was true.

This terrible period was made even worse by the fact that our lovely home, built on a secluded plot of land, was about to be sold and I had to give my pet, Elvis the duck, away because there wasn't enough room where we were moving. He was shipped off to a neighbour's house and I consoled myself it was for the best because The Lad often threatened that he was going to eat Elvis for lunch.

Mum and The Lad moved into a two-bedroom flat, and I decided that if she was going to spend all her time canoodling with her toy-boy I was going to get a life of my own. If my parents saw me as an adult, then that's what I'd be. So I got myself a job selling skin care products, which was ironic because I was covered in acne and most people in such professions are expected to slap on tonnes of foundation and look immaculate. Here I was, a skinny, spotty kid, trying to look like a sophisticated woman of the world. No wonder it didn't turn out to be a life-long career.

It was around this time that I went with Mum to visit one of her friends. I was sitting on the sofa, listening to the two women chattering when I was overcome with a bout of teenage boredom and announced I was going for a walk and would be back soon.

This turned out to be a good decision because it was the day that I met the most gorgeous man I'd ever seen. I was strolling past a house nearby and came face-to-face with a blond, tanned young guy leaning on a colourfully painted Volkswagen van. If you imagine Brad Pitt in a Levis commercial, you're on the right track.

We smiled at each other and I fled, fretting that I'd make an fool of myself, but I couldn't stop thinking about him and I headed back towards my Mum's friend's house, thinking, 'Please, God, let him be there.' And there he was, leaning on his car, his short T-shirt revealing a six-pack and his long hair swishing about in the breeze.

'That's a nice van, isn't it?' I squeaked, 'Isn't the weather warm for this time of year?' After finding out each other's names the conversation improved and I found out that he'd driven all the way from Queensland and was staying with a friend for a while. When I eventually said I said I had to go Ben asked me to meet him in the same place the next day.

'Yes please!' I almost shrieked at the top of my voice, but I stopped myself, desperately wanting to look cool.

By this time I'd joined a band as a lead singer and was deadly serious about making it in the music business, but I actually earned a living working in a cake shop, which did wonders for my skin problem.

The following day, I sold the last cream puff to an old lady and ran to the place where I'd met Ben. And there he was, as promised, waiting for me. I couldn't believe my luck: this older man (two years seemed a lot then) wanted to see me, despite my chronic zits and a chest like two fried eggs.

Ben and I spent a lot of time together and eventually decided it was time to make love. I cringe at the memory because while I was a shy virgin and Ben was quiet and unassuming, he was much more experienced than me.

My mum had always spoken of sex as if it was something to be embarrassed about, that it was dirty and not to be indulged in unless you were married. I was very tempted to bring up all the messing about she'd got up to with The Lad, but kept my mouth shut for fear of the consequences. I also recalled Mum telling me that she'd made Lucy go to the doctor to be internally examined, to check that she was still a virgin before her wedding to Robert, so it wasn't surprising that I was uptight.

My nervousness probably wasn't helped by the fact that

our first sexual encounter was in the back of Ben's van, on a single mattress. I didn't expect a swanky suite at some posh hotel, but a grope in a rickety van, down a back street wasn't what I'd read about in all those slushy girls' magazines.

In fact, I became so tense that it was impossible to do anything and I apologised over and over to Ben, thinking I'd let him down and he wouldn't want to see me again. But he was very understanding and hugged me, saying it didn't matter; that he loved me and there were other ways of making love without going all the way. However, when he told me what oral sex was I was disgusted and said, 'I'm not putting that bloody thing in my mouth!'

With Ben's encouragement, our sex life did improve, but it was far from chandelier-swinging stuff and I think there were occasions when Ben could have done with a cold shower. Ben didn't express his opinions to me about many things, but I trusted him and felt safe in his company. I soon found myself falling in love and was constantly amazed that someone so drop-dead gorgeous wanted to be with me.

Mum married The Lad and I was left to get on with it. Life was fun then with Ben, spending most of our time in the company of his best friend Sean and his girlfriend Sue. We'd enjoy barbecues on the beach and go to drive-in movies, and count how many rocking cars we could see.

I wasn't pleased that Mum had divorced Dad and married The Lad, but I was close to becoming an adult and knew her love life was none of my business any more.

When I think about The Lad now it strikes me how young and inexperienced he was and that he was looking for security and a happier home situation. I didn't know much about his life, but I do know that his relationship with his parents was difficult, and I see now that I lay too much blame at his feet and forgot that he wasn't really that much older than myself.

Not long after Mum's wedding I was out with Ben in his car and another driver shunted into the back end of the vehicle, giving me whiplash. I received a couple of hundred dollars from the man's insurance company and with the money Ben and I bought our first car together, a clapped out Volkswagen. Mum told me I had to buy The Lad some new retreads for his car because he'd given me lifts to places over the years, so I did as I was bid and then Ben and I set off for Queensland to visit his family.

But halfway there our 'new' car broke down and we were stranded in some run-down town in the middle of the bush, where the only garage was run by a grubby bloke with chronic body odour and hair that hadn't seen a bottle of shampoo in years. As Ben suspected he would, the mechanic told us our car was a clapped out wreck and would cost more to fix than the price we'd originally paid for it.

'I spent all my insurance money on this pile of crap,' I huffed to Ben, pointing an accusing finger at the car. 'That's all we need in this heat.'

'I know,' he shrugged in his usual noncommittal manner.

We left the vehicle behind and managed to hitch a lift with a man driving a truck, who dropped us off in another run-down town in the sticks. We found the sole cabbie in the area, who drove us over the pothole-ridden tracks of the outback to the nearest Greyhound bus pick-up point. It turned out that the cabbie also delivered the post and milk to all the people living in the outback; we were astounded that the milk ever made it to its destination.

The coach journey to Queensland was a long, hot one, and long before we arrived we were bursting for the loo. I was nervous about meeting Ben's parents and hoped they'd like me. Ben was my first proper boyfriend and I didn't want to make a fool of myself in front of his family. And how I wished I wasn't so damn spotty.

Ben had always been uncomfortable about discussing his parents' and changed the subject when I asked questions about them. It wasn't long before I found out why and wished I'd never suggested going to visit them.

When we finally arrived at the bus station, not too far from Ben's parents' house, his dad George was there to greet us. Although shorter than Ben, it was plain to see where he got his looks from because his father was a striking man with deep blue eyes.

Ben and George shook hands, but I noticed them exchange a wary glance at the same time. George came over to me and gave me a huge hug that I thought would break me in two.

Not long into our visit I realised that George was a religious man who liked to quote lengthy passages from the bible and preach to anyone who'd listen, ranting about 'The sins of the flesh.' This didn't stop him from having a roving eye for the ladies though and I soon found out that it was common knowledge in the area that he'd been unfaithful to his wife.

Ben's mum wasn't there to greet us and I was told that

she was in bed ill. This didn't seem to worry Ben at all and I thought it odd that he didn't go and see her as soon as we got back to the house.

I was introduced to Ben's twelve-year-old sister Katie, whom I got on with straightaway, which was just as well because I was to share a room with her as George refused to let Ben and me sleep together under his roof. Katie looked like a chubbier version of Ben, with a wide smile, but her eyes always remained sad and I felt so sorry for her.

The next morning I went into Ben's mum's bedroom to introduce myself and was faced with an unsmiling lady with hollow eyes ringed with dark shadows. It turned out that Stella had been suffering from depression on and off for many years and I was even more shocked when I saw Katie helping her mother with bed baths and other personal hygiene matters. There were occasions when I did my best to convince Stella to help herself and not keep insisting that Katie should look after her.

When I asked Stella what the matter was all she mumbled was, 'I feel down all the time. Nothing to worry about, love.'

Ben said that Stella had been in that state for as long as he could remember and that however much she tried to get the attention of his father; however much she begged, pleaded or shouted, the more George ignored her. George only had love for God and other women.

Ben talked of being four years old and sitting by his mum's bed as she lay there, not moving a muscle. He'd felt as if he didn't exist - that she had no motherly feelings for him whatsoever. He wanted her to be like his friends' mums and take him to the park and give him cuddles, but all he could see were those hollow eyes locked onto the ceiling of her room, with thick curtains blocking out the sun.

I wondered why on earth George and Stella bothered to stay together, but soon realised that they had one of those only-too-common marriages where the couple are more worried about what the neighbours would think if they divorced, than their own happiness. I wondered if my parents had done exactly the same and vowed that if I found myself in such a relationship I'd leave sooner rather than later.

Ben blamed his father for his mum's depression, the arguments they'd had over the years and the ones that continued while we were there. Ben also felt guilty about having left his mother and sister, but he hadn't been able to take the stress any more and that was why he'd gone to Adelaide.

After a month or so the atmosphere in the house began to affect me. I told Ben I was going back to Adelaide with or without him. To my horror, Ben broke down, telling me of the trauma he'd suffered as a child and that he couldn't bear to lose me. He even told me how he'd tried taking drugs just to numb his pain. I was so upset to see him in such a state and I tried to comfort him all I could, while trying not to cry myself.

The two of us agreed that we didn't want to split up and decided to return to Adelaide together as soon as we could. We bought a small van, said our goodbyes to Ben's family and were thankfully on our own once more.

We slept on a mattress in the back of the van and ate in

greasy spoons along the way, and eventually landed on my mum's doorstep, needing somewhere temporary to live, being broke after our trip. Only Mum wasn't happy to let me use my old bedroom, as she'd turned it into a TV room. But we weren't there for more than a few weeks or so and managed to find a cheap flat to rent, which Mum helped us to fund.

The place was tiny and we only had a few chairs and a bed, but it was ours and we felt grown up and independent. In fact we considered ourselves so adult that we thought it was about time we married. I was seventeen years old and although I'd had an unconventional upbringing I wasn't as worldly as I considered myself to be. Little did I suspect that I was about to learn some very hard lessons in life.

Chapter Four

Ben and I began saving for our wedding. We weren't earning a fortune but we were sensible with our cash and a nest egg began to grow.

I got a job in the company where Ben worked, welding car chassis of all things. I'd even passed a welding test under the beady eye of my supervisor, who just so happened to be The Lad. I'd known he was employed there, but I was shocked to find out he was going to be my boss. I can't say I was looking forward to working with him.

Ben had no idea what I'd been up to and I thought what a laugh it'd be to surprise him, so I told him I had a new job lined up and if I were to be offered the job he would soon know about it. The morning of my first day I got up early and made us both some sandwiches to take with us for lunch. I handed Ben his doorsteps crammed with luncheon meat and said 'Come on then, let's go to work,' walking towards the door. Ben frowned at me as I burst into laughter, before explaining my joke. He was very surprised and amused that I'd actually passed a welding test and was going to be doing the same job as him.

However, it didn't last long because I was useless. I had to stand in a pit underneath the chassis and brandish the equipment, trying to weld parts together, only the apparatus was much too heavy and bulky for my skinny body to hold onto for too long and I ended up welding big holes in the frame. There must have been lots of cars being driven about with a funny shaped chassis. Soon after I was kindly asked to leave by The Lad.

'Good,' I said, 'I never bloody wanted to work for you anyway.' With that I left.

Thinking I'd be more use where she was employed, Mum got me a position in a nursing home for the elderly. She was a nurse and I took a care assistant role. I loved chatting to the residents and doing my best to keep them occupied, but I wasn't the most organised person and it wasn't long before I made a stupid mistake.

One of my first tasks was to collect the patients' false teeth and clean them. I suppose any sensible person would have done this one pair at a time and then return them to the right person's bedside table, but I grabbed the dentures all in one go. I gave each set a scrub with special cleaning fluid and was really pleased with my efforts, until I realised what I'd done.

Instead of owning up to my lack of forethought I used guesswork and replaced the assorted gnashers on the bedside table of whom I thought they might match while the residents slept. The next day everyone woke to find that the tooth fairy had left them each a pair of alien dentures and the bells at their bedsides rang out loudly across the wards. I spent the next couple of hours dashing about with handfuls of false teeth, trying to wedge assorted sets into the mouths of their rightful owners.

That was my biggest faux pas and I settled in to the job well. Ben and I carried on putting money into our joint account and our wedding day drew closer.

My parents were paying the wedding bill, so we had to go along with what Mum wanted. Ben and I had hoped for a quiet do, but she put her foot down, saying, 'No daughter of mine has a poxy little wedding.'

The ceremony was held in a small church, the reception in a hotel and all the wedding gear was chosen by Mum, including flowers, colour schemes, music and even my wedding dress. Mum said that she'd splashed out enough so I wasn't to have the outfit that I so desperately wanted. As a little girl I'd envisioned floating down the aisle in some frilly white number with a crinoline skirt and long train. I was sorely disappointed that I had to wear a plain, borrowed dress. Mum's friend's daughter had just got married, so Mum arranged to the refit the dress to my measurements, scoffing at my protests and reminding me 'Your father and I fucking well paid for all this.'

On our wedding day Ben and I had six of our own guests and the rest of the church pews were filled with friends and colleagues of my mother's. Ben and I left the reception early and headed home to play chess with Sean and Sue, leaving Mum to be the belle of the ball. It wasn't how I imagined my wedding day to be, but I was glad to get out of that hateful dress.

Our wedding night was also a disappointment because I hoped that once I was married I'd relax about sex, even though Ben and I had already been living together. I remembered my mother telling me that any sexual act was to be indulged in only when married, but the gold band on my finger didn't seem to make any difference. I still had problems letting go and enjoying myself. I could see Ben was annoyed but he didn't say anything and after a quick fumble he went to sleep. I laid there wishing I hadn't listened to Mum and that I'd stopped her taking over our wedding.

Exactly the same happened with my sister's weddings, so I shouldn't have been surprised and I knew if I said anything to Mum she would have branded me 'an ungrateful fucking cow.' Like my father, I've never been one for confrontation and I couldn't be bothered to stand up to her.

As the years went by though I did find my voice and was no longer afraid of speaking my mind. In fact, the relationship I share with Mum continues to be difficult because of my lack of fear and her inability to see or admit her past or current wrongdoings. I don't hate my mother and forgiveness isn't an issue because whatever Mum has done is up to her to face and not for me to judge.

There have been occasions when Mum has apologised but her actions don't always reflect this and she has often denied her bad behaviour.

Sheena recalls an evening when she was fourteen and excited about going on a date with a boy she liked and actually went on to marry. Mum warned Sheena to be home by ten, but she was enjoying herself and lost track of time. Lucy said that by ten-fifteen Mum was furious, pacing up and down and yelling 'Where's that fucking black-eyed bastard?'

Mum drilled it into Lucy and Sheena that for every minute past ten they were late they'd be grounded for a week and she stuck to her word, so my sisters generally tried to be punctual; they didn't want to miss seeing their boyfriends.

Mum waited on the doorstep and at last spotted Sheena sauntering towards home, hands in pockets, showing no sign of concern. This riled Mum more and she flew down the street and grabbed Sheena, shaking and slamming her into the front of a shop. Sheena refused to plead or cry as she was dragged home and called terrible names. Lucy screamed for Mum to stop her abuse and when my mother finally calmed down Sheena looked into her eyes and asked in a quiet voice, 'Have you finished now?'

Even when Sheena was in her late forties Mum tried to undermine my sister. Sheena was extremely creative and was determined to branch out and run her own business. She saved her money until she had enough to rent a market stall in Wandsworth, selling beautiful home-sewn cushions and other crafts. Sheena was so pleased with her efforts, but Mum soon put a stop to my sister's happiness and she was shocked to find out that Mum called the council, claiming Sheena was trading illegally.

Lucy has had run-ins with Mum too, although Sheena has taken most of the abuse over the decades and has been unable to release herself from Mum's shadow. Even now that she's in her mid fifties, Sheena can't erase the past from her memory.

Mum's bad treatment of Sheena has continued, causing unease within the family. Mum outdid herself when she was involved in helping to arrange for Sheena's husband's ashes to be taken and scattered without my sister's permission. Sheena was traumatised after watching Adam die of cancer and wasn't ready to face losing him completely. Only weeks had passed since the cremation and Sheena needed to grieve in her own way and in her own time.

My sister shed a lot of tears during that period and she's always looked so sad to me ever since. Sheena has a pretty smile and she uses it often but I can tell that she's smiling for other people's benefit. She doesn't feel it inside. I hope, one day, she will.

I would like to think that if she could Mum would go back and take the opportunity to improve her mothering skills. No parent is perfect, but we were children and young women, and she was meant to be our role model, our point of reference when entering adulthood. It wasn't surprising that my sisters and I had left home and got married by the time we were eighteen. We just wanted a life of our own.

Soon after the wedding I got a job in the maternity ward of a hospital and Ben and I moved into a bigger house.

One evening we received a phone call from Ben's brother Joey, saying that he wanted to come to Adelaide and stay with us for a while. A handsome man, the spitting image of Ben, turned up looking dishevelled and his expression told me he had troubles. It was obvious he was a vulnerable soul, like Ben. Joey did appear to relax and open up after a few weeks in our home and he went out and bought himself a bright purple van with a bed in the back, which he called his 'shagging wagon'. I felt sorry for Joey and was eager to make sure he felt as welcome as possible, and Ben found his brother a job in the firm where he worked.

One night, not too long after Joey's arrival, I was woken up by shouting from the kitchen and went downstairs to see what was going on. Ben and Joey often did late shifts, so I'd

43

be fast asleep when they came home.

I walked into the kitchen to find two men, much older and bigger than Ben and Joey, pushing them around and threatening violence. One man had hold of Joey's long hair and the other was gripping Ben's arm and shaking him.

'What the fuck's going on?' I shouted.

A guy with a shaven head and bad teeth told me that Joey had raped his little sister and got her pregnant, so they'd come around to 'teach the dirty bastard a lesson he'll never forget.'

Joey tried to free himself from the man's grasp, denying everything and repeating that the girl was lying and he'd never dream of doing such a terrible thing. This just infuriated the men more and one shouted 'Don't fucking call my little sister a liar!' With that Joey's head was smashed into the wall.

Ben tried to move towards his brother but the man holding him twisted his arm viciously behind his back, making him yell out in pain. By now the noise in the kitchen was awful; threats of violence and revenge were being screamed into the ears of my husband and brother-in-law. I could envision what was about to happen and knew I had to try and do something, so I picked up a nearby saucepan and hit one of the thugs over the head with it. This didn't seem to have much of an effect and just made him angrier. The three men then bundled us into their car and drove off like maniacs.

Ben put his hand on my knee, and I could tell by his expression he was trying to say 'Everything's going to be okay.' Joey just stared straight ahead, his face showing no

44

emotion; but I think he was trying to work out how to persuade the men not to harm us. Finally, he asked them to let us go, repeating that he hadn't touched their sister and that he'd never rape a woman. Ben joined in, pleading with them to stop the car and both were answered with slaps and punches.

Some miles down the road the men stopped the car and dragged us all out and into their sister's house. She was a tiny little thing who stood there motionless and silent, not daring to look the three of us in the eye.

Unable to suppress my fury any longer I leapt forward and punched the girl in the face, knocking her to the floor and pulling her hair.

'I'm not letting you go until you tell us the truth, bitch!' I yelled.

Her brothers were too busy struggling with Ben and Joey to go to their sister's aid, and with a couple more hair tugs and threats from me she confessed that she'd made the whole story up. She'd got drunk at a party, had sex with a stranger and was pregnant. She was too ashamed to tell her parents and brothers, so she'd picked on Joey because everyone knew she'd gone out on a few dates with him.

Joey, Ben and I were disgusted that someone would make up such a story. Poor Joey could have gone to jail for years. She didn't care; she just stood there, her hair all over the place, sobbing. I wanted to give her another good slap and tell her she deserved everything she got.

The girl and her brothers didn't even have the decency to offer us an apology and shrugged the episode off as a misunderstanding. The men gave us a lift home, pushed us out of the car and warned us not to involve the police and then sped off into the night. Joey and Ben wanted to forget what happened, but I wasn't prepared to let the men off so lightly.

'Stuff them. How dare they do that to us,' I said and called the police. Nothing ever came of my complaint, which infuriated me, considering what we'd been through.

After that, Joey changed dramatically, showing no respect for either himself or others. He'd slouch around the house with a sullen expression on his face, turn up late for work, if at all, and answer in grunts when asked a question.

Not long after this episode I found out I was pregnant and Ben and I were over the moon, if a little shocked, but sadly I miscarried at nine weeks. Mum and Ben told me that it wasn't meant to be, that it was 'just one of those things', but it didn't feel like that to me at that time. I craved comfort and understanding, not so-called wise words.

Then a few months later I found out I was pregnant again and I didn't have the energy to deal with Joey's attitude any longer, so I asked Ben to get his brother to leave. Ben refused, saying it wasn't right to throw a member of his family out. I argued that Joey was causing a permanent atmosphere in our home and that we weren't just going to throw him out on the streets; he was welcome to stay until he found somewhere else. Ben wouldn't budge, so feeling irritated, I took matters into my own hands and a month later Joey found a place to live and left us to it.

I gave birth to a beautiful, healthy baby boy weighing seven pounds, who I called Shane. When the nurse passed him to me for the first time, like a million other new mothers, I was overwhelmed with love and thought how clever I was, bringing such a tiny being into the world.

Ben was with me throughout the birth and tears shone in his eyes as he held his son. We were both elated to be parents and I took to motherhood straightaway, although I went through the baby blues for a while.

So pleased was I to be a mum I couldn't wait for Ben to visit me at the hospital the day after Shane's arrival. I remember looking at my pale reflection in my compact mirror and trying to make myself look inviting by applying lipstick and blusher.

Ben's visit didn't go to plan however because he turned up with a scraggy bunch of roses that he'd taken from our own garden and he held them out to me like he was presenting me with a BAFTA.

I looked at the other new mums in my ward with their huge bouquets that filled the air with perfume and I was tempted to smack Ben over the head with my plastic water jug.

'That's all I get for straining away for twenty hours, a handful of fucking weeds. Don't push the boat out too much, will you? I wouldn't want you to break the bank,' I said.

Poor Ben's face reddened and he muttered an apology.

A few days later we took Shane home. We'd made a real effort with his nursery and filled it with soft toys and a gorgeous cot that Mum had bought. He turned out to be a good baby who fed and slept well, and was content most of the time. But our serenity didn't last long and a string of

47

events left Ben and me shaken.

One night I woke up with a crushing weight on my chest, as if someone was sitting on me. I tried to reach out for Ben to wake him up, only I couldn't move. It grew heavier and heavier until I feared I was dying, but just as I thought I'd black out the fear went and I found myself floating out of my body, reaching up towards the ceiling, then looking down at myself and my sleeping husband. Then I started hitting Ben over and over again.

'What am I doing?' I asked myself.

Moments passed and something or someone told me I had to return to my body. The next thing I knew I was sitting up in bed crying and pinching myself to see if I was still alive and I looked at Ben to check he that he was in one piece. I was confused and couldn't work out what had happened.

But that wasn't the end of it: looking into the darkness of our room I saw a man staring at me from the foot of the bed, and although he appeared to be human I knew he was a spirit. My heart was pounding and I couldn't take my eyes off him.

I shook Ben out of sleep and asked him if he could see another person in the room. Ben's eyes flickered open and focused on the foot of the bed.

'Ben,' I said in a whisper. 'Can you see him?'

My husband didn't move and was silent for a moment. Finally he answered, 'Yes, there.' He nodded towards the exact spot where the man was standing. We grabbed each other by the hand, too afraid to move or speak.

The spirit, a tall, dark middle-aged man wearing what

appeared to be a green or brown jacket continued to watch us for a little longer, smiled and then was gone.

Needless to say, we were both unnerved by the incident – particularly Ben who was an atheist and we slept with the light on for weeks.

Just as we were getting over our jitters, however, we were visited by another spirit. Ben was asleep and I was in that lovely stage between wakefulness and slumber when the most dazzling white light filled our bedroom. It wasn't a flash but a warm glow that gradually grew brighter and brighter, like the lights in a theatre that slowly flood the stage at curtain-up.

The light had no shape or beginning or end to it and it mesmerised me, making me feel happy and warm. I was without a doubt that it was there to protect me, though I don't know what from. It was one of the most memorable experiences of my life and in difficult times that ensued I often pictured the light and it was a source of comfort.

I thought long and hard about the spirit of the man and the light and had a strong feeling that I should put my experiences down on paper. I don't really know why; it was more like an urge, a hope that things would become clearer.

Not long after I found my note pad and was working out what to write when my hand started to move of its own accord, scribbling words very quickly, so quick that my hand felt as if it was out of control. I wasn't frightened; I just assumed that someone was trying to give me a message. But however hard I tried I couldn't slow my pen enough to fathom what I was writing and all I was left with were a lot of squiggles.

I went to a local spiritual church to ask their advice and they explained about automatic writing, where a spirit sends a signal or message to a living being, using the written word. They told me that I should count my experiences as gifts.

At home so many questions filled my head: what's going on? Who's trying to contact me? What do they want? Why me? On and on the questions went, yet I felt privileged and secure in the knowledge that I had nothing to worry about.

Chapter Five

Ben and I decided to buy a plot of land and build our own home, that being the fashionable thing to do in Australia in 1975. We paid a holding deposit and had eight weeks to find the remaining eight hundred dollars, which was a lot of money then.

I worked shifts in a burger bar similar to McDonald's. I hated the bright red and yellow uniform with its stupid little hat. I also carried on with my main job at the hospital; at least I had a sense of pride when I put my nurse's uniform on. The hospital had crèche facilities, which were perfect for Shane. Ben accepted all the overtime he could and we managed to get the money together before the deadline. We were only in our early twenties and were really proud of our achievement.

We arranged a mortgage on our combined salary and the builders set about constructing our dream home. Every day after work either Ben or I would visit the site to see how it was progressing, and I was so excited about the project that I'd take Dad along too. He was pleased for me and I hoped he was impressed by my determination. It seemed to me that Mum was always too busy to visit on a regular basis; she wanted to wait until there was more to see.

Three months later the house was complete and we were able to move in. We had no floor coverings, just concrete, and no lawn or fencing around the garden, but we didn't care; we were the second couple to have built a house on the development and felt very proud.

Yet things weren't going so well between Ben and me. I found his lack of social graces embarrassing, especially when people asked if we'd had a row because of Ben's unwillingness to make conversation or show interest when we were in company. I was tired of having to make decisions on my own, especially when it came down to the house and garden: Ben had lost his enthusiasm, which disappointed me, it being our first proper home and having worked so hard.

Another sore point between us was his family. Ben's mum left his dad, due to his womanising, and moved to Adelaide with Katie. They were renting a tiny house not far away from us, as Stella was on sickness benefit. She was plummeting further into depression, causing me great concern - particularly when one minute you'd be holding a reasonably normal conversation with her and the next she'd be screaming nonsense. I lost count of the times the neighbours found her shuffling around the street in her slippers, muttering or yelling loudly into thin air.

Either Ben was humiliated by his mother's behaviour or he didn't care; either way I was frustrated at his lack of support. Joey and Katie were exactly the same and avoided their mother as much as possible. Joey was getting on with his own life and Katie had met a boy and was off gallivanting with him.

When Stella locked herself in a friend's car, brandishing a pair of scissors, shredding the upholstery and shrieking 'I'm going to kill myself! Do you hear me?' I knew that drastic action had to be taken.

However hard I tried, I couldn't coax Stella out of the car, so there was no other option than to call the police. Ben and I finally agreed that Stella had to get professional help and she was taken to a psychiatric hospital in a straight jacket, which tore Ben and me apart. If I'd been informed that she was about to be given electric shock treatment I wouldn't have consented to her being sectioned. I was furious at this barbaric idea and spoke to Ben about it, and as usual, he wasn't interested, making no comment about his mum's medical care. I knew he'd had a difficult childhood, but I couldn't understand why he wouldn't visit his mum or at least ask how she was doing.

I felt so sorry for Stella when I saw her in the hospital. She sat on a chair, backed against the wall of the ward, staring straight ahead with those awful hollow eyes. She wasn't muttering or shouting and didn't look at me. In fact, I think the treatment had affected her so badly that she had no recollection of who I was or where she was. At that moment I felt really guilty for putting her in there and it played on my mind for some time to come. All of a sudden it seemed that my friends were young and carefree, while I was an old lady with the world on my shoulders.

Seeing how neglectful Ben was of his mum, I lost respect for him and was resentful that I had to cope alone.

Things got even worse when George landed on our doorstep a few months later, announcing he'd come to live with us. Knowing Ben's dad, I was well aware he hadn't come to Adelaide to see us or take care of his wife, and after much probing I found out he was on the run from the taxman, along with a few women's husbands I imagined. Ben's family were becoming a terrible burden and it got to the point where Ben was so distant and uncaring about my views that I felt like leaving home.

'I've had enough of your fucking family!' I yelled one night as I was cooking something that resembled dinner. 'I've got your mum going loony, your dad and his bible-bashing and tarting about with every bit of skirt he can get his hands on. Any more of this and I'll be joining your mum in a fucking nut house!'

It wasn't as if I was asking for much, only some peace in my own home with my small son. I had to face the fact that my marriage was on shaky ground. Once again our sex life became non-existent, except for the occasions when Ben would get desperate and plead with me to give him oral sex, promising that he'd take me out for a slap-up dinner, if I'd do it. Dinner or no dinner, that thing wasn't going in my mouth.

In an effort to escape the hardships Katie went off and married her boyfriend. I was glad that she'd found a life of her own and was able to enjoy the freedom that should come with being a trouble-free teenager. She might have been unhelpful during the time Stella was in hospital, but the girl had acted as her mum's nurse long enough.

Another Christmas came and went without a present from Ben. He said that Christmas was too commercialised and a waste of money. I didn't want gold watches or designer clothes, just a symbol of his affection for me. He did make sure that Shane had a nice time though, and we bought him new toys. Our problems didn't change how deeply Ben felt for his son.

One of my friends who worked with Ben at the factory told me I was lucky to have such a husband and it was obvious that she fancied him. I was proud that another woman found him attractive, yet I no longer had any passion for him myself. We were like flatmates and when we were home together another 'argument' would start, with me doing all the talking or yelling. I'd tried sitting Ben down and getting him to open up and discuss our problems, but it never got us anywhere and I'd just end up frustrated.

Perhaps if Ben's family had left us to get on with it our relationship may well have stood more of a chance - who knows? To be honest Ben and I were complete opposites and had nothing in common, apart from Shane.

It was painfully obvious that we needed some time away from each other. I told Ben I wanted a temporary split and although he cried and couldn't understand why, he moved into my mum's house for a while. They weren't particularly close, but I think Mum was hoping that I'd see sense and, after a good think, have Ben back. She was happy with The Lad and the last thing she wanted was a lodger spoiling her new-found marital bliss.

Shane and I had the house to ourselves and I must admit I thoroughly enjoyed the peace. I could have friends over without fretting about my husband not joining in the conversation and I certainly didn't miss the one-sided arguments and the silences. I felt free and glad to be away from the stresses that Ben's family continually threw at us. I thought of ending the marriage permanently and decided I'd take a break from Adelaide to weigh up my options. It was a big step to take and I wanted to think things through with a clear mind and no interruptions.

I'd never really settled in Australia, so I booked a flight to England, which I'd missed since the day we set sail. I hadn't seen my father's family since 1968 and was excited at the prospect of spending six weeks with them.

I told Ben of my plans and he was adamant that he didn't want me to go. He asked why I needed a holiday and I thought how selfish he was, considering the last time I'd set eyes on my family I was eleven.

Ben drove me to the airport, begging me to reconsider, and I continually assured him the break would do us both good. I may as well have been talking to myself because he refused to understand my point-of-view. It made me sad to leave Shane behind, but I knew he'd be fine with his dad and six weeks wasn't that long.

I landed at Heathrow airport and although I was exhausted, I couldn't wait to see my grandparents and uncle, who'd arranged to meet me.

Walking through the crowds with my luggage trolley, I wondered where everyone was and if we'd recognise each other, when I heard my name being called. I turned to my left and there my family were with big smiles on their faces. I burst into tears and rushed into their arms, at once feeling as if the years apart had never occurred.

Over the first few days in Britain, in between catching up on old news, I slept, and it was after that I met the woman who has been the greatest inspiration of my life. She proved to be my closest friend and most loyal ally - my father's elder sister Joyce. In fact, part of the reason I decided to write this book was to show Auntie how much I love her and to thank her for her support through the most difficult times.

I couldn't really remember much about Auntie Joyce from my childhood days; just that she was a big, kind lady with a lovely smile. She and my Uncle Victor lived near to my grandparents in Windsor and as soon as I stepped into their house I felt more at ease there than anywhere else.

Auntie was still homely looking, organising those around her and making sure everyone was comfortable and had everything they needed. She was bossy, but she had a warm character and I loved staying with her. She had one of those kitchens you never wanted to leave. It was big and had an old-fashioned Rayburn cooker. She was always fiddling about in her kitchen and the smell of freshly baked cakes hit you the minute you walked in.

That afternoon I found another old friend from the past - a local sweet shop. How I'd craved Caramacs, sherbet lemons and Spangles. I strolled back to Auntie's with a full mouth and heavy pockets.

I missed Shane terribly and spoke to him on the phone. Conversations with a child of three were limited, but it was good to hear his little voice. I tried to avoid speaking to Ben because he kept asking when I was going back to Adelaide, telling me that I shouldn't be in England. He wanted me to shorten my trip and return to Australia before the six weeks were up. Ben was aware how much I'd missed everyone in the UK and how hard I'd saved for the trip and I was annoyed he was being this way. I think if he'd been supportive and keen to see me happy I might have been more open to giving our relationship another go. Now I was sure there was no future for us.

A few weeks into my visit my aunt and uncle invited me to a ladies' night dinner dance in London. Uncle was Master for the Masons - not that I had any idea what it was all about. Anyway, the party was a special Masons do and it just so happened that I'd packed a pretty evening dress, well, it wasn't really a dress, but my nightie, only no one could tell the difference because it was very glamorous, so I thought. I was thrilled to be attending such an event, and in a posh London hotel no less. I felt like Cinderella going to the ball.

Being Master, my uncle had a chauffeur-driven car to take us to the bash and a posh limo turned up outside the house. A gorgeous young man in a suit was driving and as he opened the rear door for me our eyes met and a rush of adrenaline shot through me. It was a feeling I hadn't experienced before and while the man drove to London we shared lingering glances in the mirror. Sorry to offend you with another cliché, but it was as though we were the only two people in the car.

The young man said he was picking us up at the end of the evening and I was beside myself, wishing I could just get back in the car there and then, forget the dance.

I had a marvellous time at the do though; the men were dashing in their dinner suits and the ladies swished about in exquisite ball gowns. I danced all night and drank champagne, which was a new experience for me, being teetotal up until then. My cousin, his girlfriend and I got drunk and left the hotel to stagger around the statue Eros, laughing and being silly.

FOR CRYING OUT LOUD

I don't recall much about the journey home, except that the driver and I again shared a few meaningful glances. I assume they were meaningful, but I'd consumed a lot of champers and my vision was blurred. Whatever happened, the young man rang my aunt the following day to invite me out. I was relieved I hadn't made an idiot of myself and was flattered that he'd gone to such trouble and wanted to show me around London personally.

Jamie was so different to Ben. He was chatty, had a great charm about him, and he enjoyed taking me to interesting attractions and restaurants all over London. We also went sailing on the yacht he shared with his twin brother and he introduced me to horse riding in Wales.

Jamie was tall with dark brown hair and a fringe that flopped over his eyes. He was cute, in a boyish way, but sexy with it. I suppose he was a dead ringer for Hugh Grant, only not quite as posh.

We spent a lot of time together and eventually the inevitable happened. I didn't feel as if I was being unfaithful to Ben because we were separated and having been with Jamie I knew my love for Ben had completely died. I cared for him, but I didn't feel the same passion I'd had when we first married.

Sex with Jamie was knee-trembling and I was able to relax and enjoy it. I won't go into graphic details because my family will read this; let's just say Jamie taught me a few new tricks and I'd never experienced such intense pleasure in bed. Forget the bed socks and baby bottles; I was a new, raunchy Cheryl.

Jamie and I were inseparable and soon confessed that we

loved one another. My holiday was coming to a close though, and the thought of being parted was too much to bear. We discussed our predicament at length and decided that I'd return to Adelaide, tell Ben our split was permanent and return to England with Shane as soon as possible.

My only worry was that Ben might not let me take Shane and if that was to be the case there was no way I'd leave Australia. My son meant more to me than anyone and I wasn't prepared to live on the other side of the world from him – even though I thought I was in love with Jamie.

The day of my departure arrived and I thanked my family for making me so welcome. I was particularly sad to say goodbye to my auntie because we'd built up a strong bond and she was like a mother to me. Crying, I gave everyone a hug and a kiss and then Jamie turned up in his car and drove me to Heathrow. On the way we both cried and the tears really flowed when it was time to part and for me to board the aeroplane.

I shed many more tears on the long flight back to Oz, not only for Jamie, but because I was going to have to face Ben and hurt him deeply. The thought of ending my marriage wasn't one I was looking forward to, although it was clear to me that there was no other way and if it hadn't been for Shane I wouldn't have returned to Australia. My home was in England now.

As the plane touched down in Adelaide I felt sick and the only positive side was seeing my son rushing towards me at the airport, bawling 'Mummy!' It was wonderful to see Shane and give him a big cuddle. Ben smiled and put his arms around me, saying how pleased he was that I was home.

When we arrived home I gave Shane the sweets and toys I'd bought him and was amused to watch his blue eyes widen with excitement. He played with his gifts for an hour or so and then I read him a story and put him to bed. I wanted to speak to Ben alone.

I sat down and looked Ben in the eye and wondered, yet again, how on earth you tell someone you don't want to be with them any more; that you care for them but don't love them. The guilt and self-blame was eating away at me. I was going to take my son thousands of miles away from his father. I was going to set up home with my lover. I thought I was being a selfish bitch, but in my heart I knew it would be crueller to Ben in the long run if I pretended I was happy and that everything was okay.

'Ben, I'm going back to England. I've met someone,' I said.

But Ben did nothing. His face showed me he was hurt and shocked, but he didn't cry, shout or storm out. He was silent, even when I said I wanted to take Shane with me. He didn't beg me to stay or call me names, accusing me of being an adulteress, as you'd expect under the circumstances.

With the benefit of experience and maturity, I can see that Ben loved me very much and just couldn't find the words to tell me how he felt - that he was terrified of losing Shane and me. In the end, he probably accepted that I was unhappy with him and loved me enough to let me go. If only I'd seen behind his quietness and not mistaken it for lack of love or interest on his part. We had rushed into marriage too young and become bogged down by financial commitments and family troubles. We should have been out and about, having fun together, being carefree. I couldn't remember the last time Ben and I had shared a laugh like we had in the old days.

As it turned out, Ben had something to confess too: he'd slept with the woman he worked with, who fancied him. Ben had confided in her one night, telling her about the situation between him and me, and they'd got drunk and had sex.

I wasn't surprised or jealous. In a way, I guess it made me feel less guilty about my affair with Jamie, but Ben was disappointed that I wasn't in the least hurt.

Mum and Dad weren't happy about my plans either and warned me to think seriously about my decision. I was adamant though; Jamie loved me, I loved him and he made me feel special and wanted. When I recall that period of my life I can see that what Jamie and I shared was lust and passion. There was no real basis for a proper commitment, but when you're in those exciting first days of a relationship you don't want to concentrate on what the future might hold. You're too busy living for the moment and enjoying every second. Jamie gave me the attention I'd craved from Ben, and I was also touched that he was prepared to accept and get to know Shane.

I was only in Adelaide for ten days - long enough to file for a divorce and say my goodbyes to everyone. My friends thought I was barmy to leave my husband and head off to the other side of the world to be with someone I hardly knew.

Ben was his usual quiet self and didn't say much on the

matter, only that if he tried to stop me I'd end up hating him and he couldn't face that. He promised he'd come to the UK to visit Shane and would consider settling in England too. I was relieved about this, as my guilt over uprooting Shane and parting him from Ben was keeping me awake at night. I so wanted father and son to maintain a strong bond.

I was leaving everything behind – the house, my family, my friends and even my lovely dog. I crammed as many clothes and belongings in a couple of bags as I could and waited on the doorstep for my dad, who was taking us to the airport. It was a humid day, made more suffocating by the fact that I began to panic and my heart was beating manically. I managed to calm down by reassuring myself that I was doing the best thing for all involved.

Dad drove up to the house and Ben and I shared a farewell hug. I felt a little sadness, of course, but in all honesty it wasn't an overwhelming sensation. I was more concerned for him and could see he was battling to keep his emotions under control. Ben was brave though and didn't get upset in front of Shane. He gave his son a big cuddle and said 'Daddy loves you and will see you very soon.'

I'll never forget the expression on Ben's face as the car drove away, and although I no longer wanted to be with him, I regretted that our marriage was over and wished we could go back to happier times.

Dad said little on the way, but I knew that he was worried for my future welfare. He did say 'You have to go, otherwise you'll wonder if you've missed out on something special and end up resenting Ben.'

Mum had turned her back on me because of the break-up, which was hurtful, but the most upsetting part was saying goodbye to Dad. We swapped a hug and shed some tears and then Shane and I were off to board our plane. I turned several times and waved to my father as I walked away. He disappeared further into the distance and then, was gone.

Shane slept for most of the long flight and woke once or twice, asking where his daddy was, but soon he was in a deep slumber again. While he dozed, questions whirled around my head. Had I done the right thing? Would Jamie and I work out? Would we find somewhere to live? Would Ben move to England? I tried to sleep and stop my mind working overtime, only the more I tried the more I failed. But despite my self-reproach, deep down I was positive that I wasn't making a mistake - plus I was soon to see the man I loved. I'd already explained to Shane that we were going to meet a friend of Mummy's and that we'd stay with him and his family for a while.

Shane's eyes were wide as he asked 'Will I have a room big enough for my new toys?'

Poor little mite; I needed to find a job before I'd be able to buy him anything and make up for the fact that we'd left most of our belongings in Australia.

Jamie and I planned to find our own place as soon as possible and although he had money stashed away in his bank account, I wasn't happy about relying on him – especially not so soon into our relationship. Job-hunting was my first priority.

Walking through customs, my stomach was doing somersaults at the prospect of seeing Jamie again. And suddenly there he was with his floppy dark fringe and his gorgeous smile. We must have looked like two actors in a slow motion scene in a romantic spoof as we swept into each other's arms, me pulling a confused little boy along behind me.

'Mummy, is this your friend then?' Shane asked, frowning at the tears flooding down Jamie's and my faces.

Jamie stooped down, said hello to my son and scooped him up for a hug.

We went back to Jamie's family's home and after recovering from our jet lag went about settling into a new routine.

Shane and I spoke to Ben often on the phone and he reassured me he was fine and told Shane he'd fly to the UK soon for a visit. I was so happy to be in England and close to my dad's family, but there was one part of my new life that wasn't going so well: it didn't take at all long for me to realise that Jamie and I weren't made for each other. For the first couple of weeks the three of us enjoyed days out together, but I soon noticed that Jamie was beginning to resent the time I spent with my son. He'd question me as to my whereabouts and ask why we couldn't have more evenings on our own. He wanted our relationship to be the way it was when we first met - just the two of us pleasing ourselves. My having a small child around changed all that; Jamie grew distant and our sex life dwindled dramatically. Mums weren't supposed to be sex kittens in the bedroom, you see.

I was very upset and hoped the situation would improve once Jamie got used to Shane being on the scene, so I tried to ignore my misgivings and concentrated on Christmas.

We spent the holiday season with Auntie Joyce, Uncle Victor and the rest of the family. They did their best to spoil Shane and on Christmas morning my little boy's face lit up when he saw all his presents under the tree. He couldn't believe that Santa had brought him so many new toys.

All the usual Christmas traditions were upheld and we ate a huge dinner, pulled crackers and sipped sherry, enjoying the company of family and loved ones. It was a happy time and I persuaded myself that every new relationship needs time to settle down. Jamie and I were going to work out.

I was wrong: and after Christmas Jamie sat me down and told me that he'd made a mistake and that the responsibility of Shane was overwhelming him. I was furious; it wasn't as if I left Shane with him or expected him to adopt my son.

'I can't believe you let me move halfway around the world, give up everything I have to be with you and you tell me this!' I shouted. 'How could you do this to me?' And with that I slapped him across the face. I didn't use much force – just enough to send his floppy fringe flying across the other side of his forehead, where it wobbled and finally came to rest. Jamie wasn't bothered that I'd smacked him; all he cared about was his hair and he raised a hand to smooth down his fringe.

'You and your silly bloody hair.' I pointed, laughing. 'You're a dickhead.'

Jamie sniffed at me, raised an eyebrow and sauntered out of the room.

After I'd calmed down the truth hit me, I'd been dumped. It was a terrible blow, knowing my new life was a failure and that Jamie hadn't really loved me after all – at least not enough to accept my son as well. Now I think even if I hadn't had Shane we probably wouldn't have worked out either. Jamie liked the thought of commitment, but the real deal was another matter. He was scared stiff.

It was the New Year and meant to symbolise a new beginning for me, but all I felt was emptiness. I was lost. I told Ben that Jamie and I had split and he begged me to return to him. I refused, aware that even if I did go back to Australia I couldn't carry on with our marriage.

My next problem was finding a job and a place to live, but going backwards wasn't an option. I had to try and keep positive for Shane and myself. I told Ben that my life was in England now and he sounded sad, so I encouraged him to come over and visit as soon as possible. This seemed to cheer him up and he agreed to book a flight when he could afford it.

That was the last time I spoke to Ben. On 10th January 1979 I was told Ben had hung himself. He was just twenty-five years old.

Chapter Six

'Ben's dead. He's fucking dead! He hanged himself from the loft in your fucking house!' Mum shouted down the phone from Adelaide. 'You murdered him! It's your fault for leaving him. You killed your husband, you fucking hear me?'

I started to shake, unable to take in the news.

Shane and I had been at the shops when Jamie and his parents received the dreadful news from Mum, and when I got back they told me to call Adelaide immediately.

My stomach lurched as I dialled my mum's number, fearing that something had happened to Dad or one of my sisters. It was then that Mum gave me the worst news I'd ever heard in my life, in the cruellest manner imaginable.

Over and over she ranted and blamed me for Ben's death. Over and over she bellowed, 'You'll pay for this! You fucking murderess!'

Ben dead? He couldn't be. I looked at Jamie and then I turned to his parents. Finally, my eyes rested on the family doctor, who'd come to offer any support he could. Surely they'd got it wrong and Ben was at work or fiddling with the engine of his car. But no, their faces told me that it was the truth and that my husband was, in fact, dead.

I don't know if I screamed. I don't remember if I fell to my knees or said anything in particular. I do remember the room beginning to spin and feeling unsteady on my feet, and I'm sure someone put their arm around me and led me to the sofa. At a certain point during the commotion I'd dropped the phone receiver, leaving my mother to yell accusations at no one.

The doctor offered me a sedative tablet, which I refused. Instead I grabbed my little boy's hand and announced that I was going to my grandparent's house. All I wanted was to see a friendly face: someone I knew would be some form of comfort to me.

Jamie tried to follow and put his hand on my arm, but I was in such shock that I pushed him away, rudely telling him where to go.

I made it to my grandparents' house and managed to find the words to tell them what had happened. They did their best to console me, but I couldn't take anything in. I was numb, unable to speak or cry.

Shane peered closely at me, knowing that his mummy wasn't well, so I hugged him and wondered how I could make a boy of three understand that his daddy was dead and he'd never see him again. How would I explain in years to come that his father had taken his own life? I wanted to go to sleep and not wake for a long, long time – not until someone shook me out of my nightmare to tell me Ben was alive, that it had been a misunderstanding, a sick joke.

I was sitting on my grandparents' sofa, half-listening to their words of comfort, sipping their tea and trying to make sense of what had happened when Auntie Joyce came into the room. Without uttering a word she just held me. I was glad to have her near and Auntie continued to be my strength over the months and years that followed. She not only offered me a listening ear; she opened her home to my son and me. If it wasn't for the unending support of Auntie

Joyce, my Dad's other sister Peggy and her husband Bert I don't know where Shane and I would have ended up.

Days after Ben's death, Jamie and I split for good and Auntie made room for us in her home. How she managed to keep strong for Shane and me during that time I'll never know because some disturbing actions were about to badly affect our daily lives.

Over in Australia Mum was rallying her troops and abusive phone calls and poison letters started to arrive at Auntie Joyce's. Mum would send me long letters accusing me of deliberately killing my husband and being a 'fucking murderess.'

Not satisfied with phone calls and letters, Mum got Lucy on her side. Lucy's notes were filled with similar accusations and she even scribbled swear words over the envelope so the postman and my family could see them, adding to my shame.

Years later Lucy explained that Mum had fed her lies and fuelled her anger towards me, inciting her to write the letters. Yes, Lucy did have a mind of her own and has apologised for her part in the hurt she caused, but when Mum was focused on an issue she'd never give up.

'I'm sorry to be such a nuisance,' I'd say to my aunt and uncle. 'I'll find somewhere else to live.' But they were adamant that they'd support me all they could and didn't want Shane and me to go.

'You're family, love,' they'd remind me, 'like our own daughter.' My aunt and uncle were furious that my mother could be so nasty and vindictive and were astonished by her behaviour.

Unfortunately Lucy wasn't Mum's only recruit; her friends in Adelaide joined in too. I'd pick up the phone to hear shouts of 'You fucking murderess! You killed your own husband! Do you realise what your mother is going through?'

As if I didn't feel bad enough. Although I hadn't put the rope around Ben's neck and forced him to take his own life, I did feel terribly responsible. A thousand times I wished I'd stayed with him, even though I didn't love him as a wife should love her husband. A thousand, no, a million 'what ifs?' kept me in a permanent state of stress and sleeplessness, pacing my room, unable to hold a normal conversation or think about anything other than my part in Ben's death.

Auntie reassured me that it wasn't my fault, reminding me how unhappy I'd been with Ben and trying to persuade me that all I'd done was try to make a better life for myself. But I couldn't stop the awful pain that was turning me into a mental and physical wreck. Over the following year my weight fluctuated dangerously from six and a half to eleven and a half stone.

How would Shane cope without a dad? What would Ben's parents do without him? *Was* it my fault? I'd spend hours torturing myself with questions, but the answers never came.

It was Dad who called to tell me when and where Ben's funeral was to take place. I wanted to fly back to Australia and attend the ceremony, but my father warned me not to because my mother was on the warpath, threatening violence towards me if I showed up. Dad, in a sad voice, informed me that Joey was also out for my blood and didn't want me at his brother's funeral. Shane and I stayed in England; the only token of our sorrow were some flowers I sent to the cemetery.

Now when I think of this time, I wish I'd stood up to my mother and attended the ceremony, shown my respect for Ben, but I was scared of what would happen and I didn't want the day ruined for Stella and George. They had enough to cope with.

It turned out that my absence was viewed as a lack of grief over Ben's suicide, causing Mum and Lucy to step up their hate campaign. Mum was particularly angry that it was The Lad who'd found Ben dead and much later Lucy told me what happened on that fateful afternoon.

She said that no one had seen or heard from Ben for more than three days and he hadn't turned up for work either. Ben had been upset because my birthday card to him arrived late. The Lad went around and banged on the door of our house in Adelaide, but got no answer. He glanced through the glass panel of the front door and saw what he thought was Ben just standing there, unmoving. The Lad knocked and shouted through the letterbox, asking to be let in, but there was no sound from inside. Worried, he broke down the door, to be met by the sight of Ben hanging from the loft, a rope around his neck. His suicide note was found nearby, covered in blood. I didn't find out until many years later that a note existed or what it said because my mum withheld if from me for reasons only known to herself.

FOR CRYING OUT LOUD

I got through each day as best as I could, simply existing and trying not to let my thoughts dwell on my part in Ben's suicide. I had a son to support and care for after all, and part of caring for Shane was keeping him fed and clothed, so I needed money. I didn't have a job and wasn't in the right state of mind to be pounding the pavements for work, so I had no choice but to ask my mother to oversee the sale of Ben's and my home. I'd much rather have elected my dad as power of attorney but he said he didn't feel up to it.

I think Mum liked being in such a strong position, especially being on the other side of the world, and enjoyed having an influence on my future. Although she'd sent the letters, she was still my mother and I was naïve enough to trust her when it came to sorting out my financial affairs. How wrong I was. My home was sold, along with its contents, and our insurance policies cashed in. Rather than receiving the thousands I assumed I was owed, I was mailed a cheque for the British equivalent of one hundred and fifty pounds.

I hired a solicitor to handle my case and to look into what had happened to the money, but Mum said that any funds from the house were used to pay off debts. This I couldn't understand. Ben had been careful with his finances and I was no spendthrift. We'd saved for years, making sure we lived in a nice home and putting money in the bank often. Considering we'd both been so young, we were very sensible when it came to such matters.

I was well aware that Ben's insurance policy amounted to ten thousand dollars and when I asked what had happened to this Mum said that it was used to cover the expense of the funeral and our 'debts'. There was no way a funeral could amount to such a sum in 1979 and Mum made matters worse by refusing to send me any documentation related to Ben's and my personal effects. Events were cloudy around this period and Mum changed her story several times, swearing that the policy wasn't in fact cashed in. I still don't know for sure what happened to my money.

My solicitor couldn't come up with an answer either so I stopped questioning Mum, even though I was positive that she was hiding something from me. This time she'd gone too far and I decided to stay away from her.

Here I was, at twenty-three, a widow with a small son, no money and no home of my own. It was just as well I lived the other side of the world because I don't think I'd have been responsible for my actions.

Chapter Seven

I was still reeling after my recent experiences, and my guilt over Ben's death played on my mind continually, but Shane needed me to keep myself together and Auntie Joyce did her best to bolster my spirits.

During these times I spoke to God a lot and he seemed to answer me, because I found a little of my old willpower again and managed to pull myself together enough to go out and find a job in a shop. My bank account was empty so it was a relief I was earning, even if my wages didn't add up to much. I also wanted to give my aunt and uncle a small amount towards the bills, hating to be reliant on them when they'd already done so much for us.

Auntie was pleased to look after Shane while I was working, which entailed selling anything from T-shirts to slippers. It wasn't my idea of a great career move, but I didn't have any choice. My hopes of being a lead singer in a band were as strong as ever, but it appeared that Top of the Pops was going to have to wait.

Auntie Peggy and Uncle Bert were also really caring people and offered to put Shane and me up, so I jumped at the chance, concerned that I'd outstayed my welcome at Auntie Joyce's. Such a thought wouldn't have crossed her mind, but I was relieved that I had the chance to give her and Uncle a break.

Aunt Peggy's house was big and impressive, with a swimming pool in the garden. Even little Shane couldn't believe his eyes and I'm sure if I hadn't had my hand on his shoulder he'd have jumped into the pool, clothes and all.

My aunt and uncle's daughter Tara was pretty with long blond hair and a great figure. Although we got on well I always felt insecure around her and tried to bury my feelings of inadequacy. She was only a few years younger than me and here she was with two lovely parents who loved each other, a great home and many friends. I didn't resent her for her lifestyle: I just couldn't help comparing myself to her. I was a young widow with no mother to speak of, no qualifications and a child to bring up alone. I tried not to, but I feared for the future.

It wasn't long after when Sheena came up with an idea that she thought might change my nomadic life. She and her family hadn't taken to Australia and had returned to the UK five years before. I'd visited her on many occasions and was glad that we were spending time together. Even though her and Adam had four children she suggested that I move in with them, so that I had more chance of being housed by the council, due to overcrowding.

I was keen to give my dad's side of the family a break from my troubles, so I thanked my aunt and uncle and took Sheena up on her offer, contacted the council and asked them to put me on their housing list.

I did feel awkward at Sheena's place though, because I found out that she and Adam had heated arguments about me. Sheena had been disgusted by Mum and Lucy's hate campaign and had had no part in it, but she thought my decision to leave Ben and move in with Jamie was wrong and she made her views clear.

'You're a silly bloody cow, Cheryl,' she'd say, pointing a

finger at me. 'Fancy giving up a bloke like Ben. Look what a bloody mess you've made of everything!'

Adam, on the other hand, was fed up with the whole saga and had said to Sheena, 'It's nothing to do with you. Keep your nose out. It's Cheryl's life, not yours.'

Sheena was always and still is a worrier; if she forgot to worry one day she'd have a damn good worry about that. She was only looking out for my welfare and was concerned that I'd made the wrong choices. She was right – I had made a mess of everything.

Soon I was placed in a hotel for people waiting to be housed, which was the usual procedure for families in my situation. Shane and I shared a small room on the ground floor that was sparsely furnished with two single beds, a wardrobe, dressing table, and in the corner was an old enamel sink. Although the hotel itself was presentable, there were some strange characters living there. One guy had such bad body odour that you had to stay ten feet away from him otherwise you'd keel over. A few of the other men would glare as I walked by and make me feel uneasy, and there were several couples who thought it great entertainment to scream at each other endlessly.

There were times when I lay in bed at night and sobbed, asking myself how I'd managed to end up in such a mess. But my self-pity didn't last long when I reminded myself that I wouldn't be in the hotel forever. Something good was going to happen.

And it did: My father came for a visit. He'd missed Shane and me and although he was overjoyed to see us, his face fell when he clapped eyes on the hotel. He couldn't accept that his daughter had gone from owning a lovely home in Adelaide to living in a dingy room. He also expressed shock by how much weight I'd put on. I must have weighed eleven stone, which was a lot for someone of my height.

Dad's family had clubbed together to pay his airfare, so he didn't have much spare cash, but he handed me ten pounds. I was over the moon and my first thought was that I could splash out on a new iron. I was fed up with Shane and I walking around in wrinkly clothes, looking like tramps. Isn't it funny, the things you get excited about when you're broke? I cherished that iron.

It was sad saying my farewells to my dad again, but we both had lives to get on with and the hotel wasn't the most welcoming place for visitors: the owner maintained strict rules and all the residents had to leave the premises by ten in the morning and not return before four in the afternoon. I lost count of the hours Shane and I spent in the park, with me pushing him on the swing and watching him shriek with delight as he careered down the slide, scuffing the backside of his already threadbare trousers.

We'd spend hours nursing cups of cold tea in greasy spoons, playing 'I Spy', or window-shopping in town. For a treat I'd take Shane to a toyshop and let him have a good play, while keeping a beady eye out for the shop assistants. Shane always went home empty-handed, but he didn't complain or ask why he couldn't keep the Action Man or Lego bricks. Although he was just three, I think he was more than aware that his mother was in trouble.

At the end of a day trudging the streets we'd sometimes visit Sheena and Adam, until it became obvious that they'd been arguing about me again. It seemed that I was the cause of everyone's unhappiness.

'I wish everyone would piss off and leave me alone,' I'd mumble to myself constantly.

After several months I'd had enough of waiting to be housed and, having spoken to people in the same situation as me, I came to realise that it could be years before I was given a decent place to live. I'd remain on the council housing list, but I wanted out of the hotel.

A friend of mine knew a young woman in Reading who had a spare room that she was keen to rent out, so Shane and I moved again. It turned out to be a bad decision because the council estate on which Kris and her husband lived was in a trouble spot, overrun with drug dealers and noisy kids.

The room I was renting was tiny and Shane and I had to share a mattress on the floor. Once again, I spent nights lying awake wondering why I kept making the wrong decisions and hoping for a more positive future.

Kris was a friendly girl and we got on at once, but her husband Fred was lecherous and every time she left the room he'd try to kiss or touch me. He had strikingly unusual looks, which added to his air of menace: he was West Indian with piercing, light green eyes, shaped like a cat's. At every opportunity he'd stare at me, raising his eyebrows in a suggestive way and grinning stupidly. Whenever Kris was out of earshot he'd lean close to me and tell me that 'Black men's cocks are much bigger than white men's,' lowering his gaze to his crotch region and licking his lips.

I told Kris what her husband was up to, but she was besotted with him and said that her Fred wasn't the kind of person to act like that. In the end I fitted a lock to my door, in case Fred took it upon himself to come into my bedroom in the middle of the night.

Fred wouldn't give up though and soon there was an occasion when Kris was out and he came into the kitchen, as I was making breakfast for Shane. He stood, staring at me, his arms on his hips and a grin on his face. I tried to look nonchalant and carry on with what I was doing, but Fred drew closer, his breathing was heavy and his eyes were going up and down my body. I stopped cooking and faced him.

'What do you want now?'

'You know you want it,' he said. 'Go on, admit it, you're fucking dying for it.'

'In your dreams, ' I laughed.

Fred sneered and clenched his fists at his sides. I knew I had to take action and grabbed a knife from the work surface behind me, pressing the blade against his stomach.

'You come near me and I'll stab you. I fucking mean it, Fred,' I warned.

He backed off immediately, laughing and accusing me of lacking a sense of humour. I replied that his intimidation wasn't funny, but he carried on smirking.

'You know what you are? A miserable cow,' he said and left the room.

Shaking, I ran to the phone to ring Sheena, who reassured me that everything would be okay and advised me to keep hassling the council until they housed me. I didn't want to go back and live with her again, being the cause of her and Adam's rows.

After I put the phone down, Shane announced that he wanted to go out and play in the playground with the other kids on the estate. I wasn't worried about letting him go because most of the children were older than him and the area was right on the middle of the estate and could be seen from Kris's balcony. I was glad of the peace actually and wanted some time to myself to think about my next plan of action and finding a job.

So deep were my thoughts that half an hour had gone by. Jumping up, I ran to the balcony, but Shane was nowhere to be seen. Frantic, I sped down the steps and outside into the playing area. I yelled Shane's name and asked the other kids where he was and they told me he was in the sand pit. I rushed towards where the pit was placed and was horrified to find no trace of my little boy. I began to cry, screaming Shane's name as loudly as I could. All sorts of terrible images ran through my mind and my panic rose even more.

Hearing my cries, some of the other mothers came to my aid and helped me look for Shane, checking behind the flats, on the stairwells and anywhere we could think of, only there was no sign of him. The other mums tried to comfort me, saying he'd turn up when he was hungry, but I was so frightened I couldn't listen to them.

Back upstairs in Kris's flat I called the police. I paced up and down the room and returned to the balcony countless times, praying for a sign of my son. Other little children played on the swings or hauled themselves up and down on the seesaw, chattering and giggling, but Shane wasn't among them.

It must have been fifteen minutes before the police turned up, yet it seemed like forever and I was worried that the longer they left their search the worse the situation would become. But I kept myself as calm as I could and managed to give them a statement, telling them what Shane looked like and how he was dressed. I also handed them a recent photograph.

It was three hours before the police turned up with Shane, who was unhurt, although a damn sight grubbier than when I'd last seen him. It turned out that he'd decided to go for a stroll in the nearby woods because he'd got bored when the older kids refused to play with him. I thanked the police and lifted Shane in my arms, hugging him as he squirmed and moaned. I wasn't sure whether I wanted to mother him half to death or tell him off for disappearing. I didn't let him out of my sight for a long while afterwards.

That night I locked us in our room again and vowed to return to the council early the next morning to find out how my housing application was going. It was only a matter of time before Fred made another move.

The following morning I was standing in the long queue at the council offices, surrounded by other stressed out mothers with small children, when I got into a conversation with the woman next to me, who'd looked as if she'd been through the mill more than a few times.

We got on very well and I told her why I was desperate to be housed; she answered that she and her husband were broke and that she'd be pleased to rent out her spare room to me for a reasonable price. I thanked her, rushed home and packed Shane's and my gear, said goodbye to Kris and made my way to our new home. Chloe and her husband were very welcoming and though Shane and I were in a tiny room and still sharing a single bed we were safe and warm.

But I didn't feel right within myself. Nothing seemed to touch me anymore: and it was as if I'd lost the ability to feel emotion. I was just existing and waiting for each day to end so that I could block out my life with sleep. Nothing made me happy and nothing made me sad, and the weight was dropping off me at an alarming rate. Both my aunties voiced their concern, but I made light of the matter, not wanting to cause them more worry.

I'd worked myself up into such a state that I went to my doctor, intending to ask for a prescription for Valium or some such drug to calm me down. But that doctor proved to be more help than any drug I could have taken and I shall always be grateful to him. He sat there as I cried and told him of Ben's death, my mother's campaign and my living conditions, not saying a word, showing any pity or making judgements. He nodded once or twice and fiddled with his pen, but he didn't interrupt and just let me vent my distress. Then he paused for a second, leant towards me and uttered these words in his gentle Scottish accent:

'Listen, lassie. When someone decides to take their own life it's their choice, no one forced your husband to put that rope around his neck and hang himself. People take their own life because they cannot cope with *their* pain. Now, you have a wee child to bring up so are you going to sit there feeling sorry for yourself and take the blame forever or do you want to stop all this nonsense? Get your crying over with, get off your backside and get yourself a job and look to the future. That way you'll prove to those you feel you've let down that you're not the person they think you are – and more importantly who *you* think you are.'

I thanked God for that doctor. I strode out of his office with a renewed faith in myself. He was right: I could do it. I wasn't a bad person. So what if my mother and certain others thought I was wicked? In my heart I knew I wasn't and that was what counted. I was going to find a job and a new life for Shane and me.

Chapter Eight

As I walked towards the building where my first interview was about to be held, my legs shook. It wasn't a high-flying job – just a sale's assistant role selling cosmetics in a department store but it was a start.

The interview went well and I was told I was to go on a training course in London the following Monday, before I could begin working in the store. I went back to Chloe's and told her the news, relieved that I'd have money in my pocket. Chloe was pleased for me; she'd just begun child minding, so we arranged that she'd look after Shane while I was at work.

The other girls on the course and I had such fun together, and it struck me how strange it was to hear my own laughter again. I noticed I had quite a fetching chuckle, in fact. I felt like a woman in her twenties, rather than someone much older.

The week's course went by in a flash and I passed with a high grade so I returned to Reading and began working in the department store. I liked it there and I reached my sales targets, but most of the other women were older and didn't invite me out when they arranged pub nights or gatherings in their homes. A young widow was a threat to them, so I decided to start going out on my own to a local club. Many a bloke would slur into my ear 'What's a nice girl like you doing on your own?'

'I was waiting for a mate, but she hasn't turned up,' I'd reply before slinking off.

I loved to dance, but when the slow records serenaded young couples as they smooched, or groups of girls giggled together, I felt lonely. Then I remembered the words of the doctor and would forbid myself from getting depressed. I'd meet people soon enough.

I was right. While I was busy spraying the general public with eau de cologne a young man kept coming up to the counter for advice on perfume for his girlfriend. The other staff members said he really liked me, but I didn't believe them; I knew he wasn't single and my confidence was low so I doubted a man would look at me twice.

The man introduced himself as Luke and eventually admitted that his girlfriend was non-existent; he'd invented her as an excuse to talk to me. I was flattered that someone would go to such lengths to chat me up. He asked me if I'd like to go for a drink during my lunch hour and after much deliberation I agreed, though I wasn't ready for a relationship.

We had a lovely time on our first date and I mentioned Luke's uncanny resemblance to Sting. He laughed and said he'd been stopped on the street many times and asked for his autograph. The hour seemed to fly by as we swapped information about our lives; Luke was twenty-seven and from Gloucestershire and was in Reading because of his work as a labourer. I told him all about Shane and he said he'd like to meet him.

After a few more dates I introduced Shane to Luke and was impressed with my new boyfriend's way with children, watching as Luke spoke to Shane in a sensible manner, rather than in the patronising way some adults do.

He made a fuss of me too, complimenting me on how nice I looked and turning up with little gifts. I considered him a perfect gentleman and couldn't believe what luck I had, finding him. My confidence grew and I stopped making derogatory comments about myself, especially as Luke would remind me that I wasn't worthless or stupid. He'd take my face in his hands and say I was beautiful and smart, and then, a month into our romance came the words 'I love you.' I returned the sentiment.

I thought about Ben constantly and the guilt was still there, but I knew I couldn't live in the past. I was young and it was obvious that I'd meet and fall in love with another man at some point in my life.

Before long Luke proposed, and I accepted straightaway, though secretly, I had deep misgivings: I enjoyed my independence and wasn't sure I was ready to live with someone yet. Then I thought of Shane, without a father and in need of stability, and my grandparents' and Auntie's high opinion of Luke. I buried any negative thoughts and the wedding was booked.

But again those misgivings stayed with me, and a week before the ceremony I had an urge to call it off. I didn't doubt my feelings for Luke, so I put it down to my being wary of commitment and reminded myself that I should consider myself lucky, landing such a catch. If I was in the same predicament now I'd wait until I was one hundred percent sure or end the relationship altogether.

However hard I tried, I couldn't shake off the feeling of unease and I soon realised that someone was trying to get a message to me. I could feel a presence following me, and it grew stronger on the morning of my wedding day. As I was getting dressed I felt a hand come from behind me and tug at my headdress and veil. I spun around to see who was there, only to find that I was alone. I was disturbed, but had a strong feeling that it was Ben trying to get through to me, and I tried to convince myself he was congratulating me and wishing me the best for the future. Pushing my doubts to the back of my mind, I got on with the day's events.

It wasn't a lavish wedding, as Luke and I were far from well off, but my grandparents and Auntie helped out and we held the ceremony in Windsor, and had our reception at Auntie Joyce's house. My proud Granddad gave me away, smart in his best suit and blue tie.

Luke and I couldn't afford a hotel during our honeymoon in Devon and slept in his car, which I found incredibly romantic, the two of us staring out of the rusty Ford Escort's window, admiring the stars and the view across the harbour as we chomped our fish and chips.

After the honeymoon we collected Shane from Auntie Joyce and drove up to Gloucestershire to stay with Luke's sister until we found permanent jobs and a place to live. Luke's parents weren't far away and offered to take care of Shane while I worked.

I became quite close to Luke's younger sister Ellie, and some time later she blurted out a secret that her and her family had been hiding. She told me that their father sexually abused her and her sister when they were growing up. It had begun when they were no more than toddlers and carried on until both girls were in their teens and able to leave home.

FOR CRYING OUT LOUD

Ellie was sure that their mother knew what was going on but their mother carried on with her life, pretending everything was normal, and Luke never indicated that he was wise to the situation either. He certainly didn't discuss it with me.

I asked Ellie why she hadn't gone to the police, but she said she couldn't face the shame of standing up in court and having to go into graphic detail about what her father had done to her. I was shocked because I'd got on well with her parents. I didn't know what to think or do and Ellie didn't talk about the abuse again. No one did.

Luke and I got married in November 1980 and before we knew it Christmas was upon us. We hadn't secured any work yet, but I managed to scrape enough money together to buy a few gifts and a turkey and trimmings.

Ellie was celebrating the holiday season elsewhere and had been kind enough to put her tree up, along with all the other decorations. We had the run of the place and I was excited about Luke's and my first Christmas together as husband and wife.

Shane's face was flushed and wide-eyed as he opened his presents, the biggest one being a yellow truck, which he fell in love with at once. I turned to Luke, expecting him to be smiling too, but he was frowning at me and shaking his head. I asked him what was wrong.

'How come you spent so much money on *him*? Didn't you think about me?'

'But Shane's just a child. I wanted Christmas to be special for him,' I answered, shocked that a grown man would be so petty.

'And you didn't want to make it special for *me*?' Luke continued, his lip curling.

I couldn't be bothered to answer such a ridiculous question and walked to the kitchen to cook lunch, but Luke followed me, grabbed the turkey I was about to put in the oven, threw it on the floor and hit me across the face so hard that I thought he'd broken my jaw. My reflex was to protect myself by shielding my face with my hands and I backed towards the kitchen counter.

He came towards me, shaking his finger and screaming, 'Why did you fucking belittle me? Why are you trying to make me feel inadequate? I should've bought the fucking presents. I'm the man. I'm supposed to provide for my fucking family – not you! Bitch!'

I tried to make him see that he was being unreasonable and that I'd intended Christmas to be special for the three of us, but I couldn't get through to him. He started to push me around the kitchen, into the table and against the work surface, and then smacked me a few more times. Then all of a sudden he seemed to snap out of his trance-like state, saw the tears streaming down my face and crumpled to the floor crying and apologising. He kept repeating that he'd felt bad because he couldn't buy Shane and me the gifts we deserved and that he was frustrated about being so poor.

I didn't know what to think. I'd never been hit by a man and was shocked by his actions. I asked him in the calmest voice I could manage, 'Have you done this before, Luke?' He shook his head and broke into fresh sobs, begging me to forgive him and swearing it would never happen again.

FOR CRYING OUT LOUD

Shane came into the kitchen crying, upset by the noise, so I knelt down and explained that Luke and I had just been playing a game and were being silly; that there was nothing to be worried about. This seemed to calm him and off he went to push his truck around the living room. I didn't look at my husband or dare utter another word. I picked up the turkey from the lino, wiped it over with a cloth, put it in the oven and left the room.

Chapter Nine

Luke and I carried on as if Christmas hadn't happened. I made polite small talk and he answered me in short sentences, as if he were neither interested nor disinterested. He didn't bring up the fact that he'd hit me and it appeared that he'd forgotten the event had taken place. I told myself that my husband had had some kind of lapse and that if we gave each other a little space then everything was going to be like it was before, when we first met.

It had become clear to me that now we were married Luke felt he didn't need to make an effort to do anything to please me. He was short-tempered with Shane, telling him to keep quiet and not make so much noise with his toys. That really angered me; it was bad enough that he picked on me, but I didn't want him having a go at Shane.

'Leave Shane alone. He's just playing,' I'd say.

'All you care about is that fucking kid!' He'd yell, making Shane cry and run to me for a cuddle.

Another worry was that Luke was unable to hold down a job. He'd go for an interview, be offered the position, start work and then get sacked within a few days or hours. His bad attitude and lack of patience were obviously alienating his employers.

At that point I knew nothing of his family's past and I was happy that Luke's parents were still keen to take care of Shane, so I could look for a job, but the three of us were soon moved into bed and breakfast accommodation, before we could be housed by the council.

FOR CRYING OUT LOUD

Yet again Shane and I were tramping the streets, window-shopping and playing on the swings, but this time we had Luke in tow. It was a horrible reminder of being back at the hotel and of all those unsavoury characters who'd surrounded us, yet I found myself wishing I were back there with just my son. I was sure I'd made a mistake marrying Luke, but I didn't want to admit it to myself or anyone else. When Auntie called I put on my happiest voice and reassured her that life was hunky dory.

After some months the council gave us a fairly presentable, three-bedroom house in Gloucester. We didn't have much furniture or many belongings, but I scrubbed the place clean and we did the best we could with the money we had between us. I hoped that now we had our own home Luke would revert to the easy-going person he was when I was dating him.

This wasn't to be. Within the first week in our new home Luke got angry with me for not cooking his favourite dinner or for burning it; I can't remember now. Considering Luke was out of work I wanted to tell him to get off his backside and cook for himself or do other chores around the house. But I kept my mouth shut, knowing any comeback would send him into a rage - only he was already working himself up over nothing.

'This place is a fucking dump!' Spit flicked between Luke's lips. 'You're a lazy bitch!' He belted me around the face, sending me flying into the sink and banging my ribs, and then he kicked me in the leg and punched me in the jaw. I slumped to the lino, covering my face with my arms.

'Luke, leave me alone!' I screamed. 'Why are you doing

this?'

'Because you're fucking useless!' A heavy boot slammed into my ribcage. 'You stupid, ugly fucking bitch!' The sole of his shoe landed on my face and my skull was bounced into the ground.

'Stop, Luke! Please!' The pain in my head was incredible and I could feel a warm liquid seeping from a split in my lip, so I just curled into a ball and prayed that I'd get through it alive.

Similar incidents followed and now there were no apologies, just sneers and personal insults.

'What are you doing on the floor, you stupid fucking bitch?' he'd laugh after he'd kicked me to the ground. He knelt over me as I cried in pain, and whispered, 'Oh, did you have a little accident? You're a clumsy bitch, aren't you, Cheryl? A stupid, clumsy, ugly, useless fucking bitch.'

The humiliation was soon taken into the bedroom. Luke would sit on the end of the bed, order me to undress and as I did so, sneer and point at parts of my body. He'd constantly remind me that he was doing me a favour by 'fucking' me and that no one else would because I was so 'fucking skinny, ugly and flat chested.'

One day he even made me go out and buy a push-up bra, saying I was repulsive and didn't have big enough breasts to make him want to make love to me. He said I had to wear the bra in bed so he could pretend I was a proper woman.

'You've got tits like two walnuts in sacks,' he'd laugh as I tried to cover myself with my hands, dreading what lay ahead and praying it would be over as quickly as possible, as I lay there with him heaving above me.

FOR CRYING OUT LOUD

As time went on I was too scared to open my mouth, in case I said the wrong thing and ended up with a smack or a punch. Luke would constantly accuse me of looking at him in the wrong way or undermining him and his masculinity.

One night, when Shane was in bed, Luke came out of the bathroom as I walked past. He was in a terrible mood and I made some innocent comment about something or other, I don't recall what it was. He grabbed me by the hair and dragged me into the bathroom.

'You're a piece of fucking shit!' he shrieked. 'Shit should be treated like shit!'

Delving into the toilet bowl, he pulled out a handful of his recent bowel movement and wiped it right across my face, then threw me to the floor and stormed out, leaving me to clean the mess off with a flannel.

But our married life was to take a greater turn for the worse; I found out I was pregnant, and instead of being pleased at the news Luke became even more angry, probably due to the fact that another child was going to take my attention away from him.

As my baby grew inside me so did the violence. 'Luke!' I'd scream, 'don't hurt the baby! I'm begging you! Stop!'

'Shut it, bitch!' he'd yell and hurl me to the floor, before beating me about the body. I'd curl up into a ball with my arms around my knees, hoping to shield my unborn child.

One day I noticed severe bruising on Shane's face and arm and I knew that Luke was responsible, but when I asked Shane what had happened his scared blue eyes looked up at me and he said 'I was playing and I fell.'

Although I was furious I didn't want to antagonise Luke,

so when Shane was at nursery school I brought up the subject of his injuries as subtly as I could, but at the mere mention of Shane Luke went berserk and punched me over and over until I slumped to the floor, almost blacking out. It was then that I felt his heavy boot ram into my stomach.

'Stop…Luke…the baby…' I moaned as blood spilled from my mouth and nose and dripped onto the lino, my arms and knees curling around my belly. I felt another stamp in the stomach and heard as I wavered between consciousness and unconsciousness, 'How fucking dare you accuse me of touching Shane, you fucking whore!'

Luke's hands went around my neck and I could feel his whole weight bearing down on me as he squeezed hard. Choking sounds gurgled from my throat and I tried to breathe but his thumbs were digging deeply into my windpipe. I had no energy left to struggle or attempt to push him off and I slipped into blackness.

When I came around Luke was gone. I dragged myself from the floor and looked at my face in the bathroom mirror. Both eyes were swollen; purplish bruising covered my jaw and cheekbones and my neck was ringed with fingerprints.

I wiped the blood from my mouth and nose with a flannel, had a glass of water, spitting blood down the sink and, as best as I could, walked to Shane's nursery school to pick him up. I knew I had to get away from Luke as soon as I could, before he killed me – or even worse, my son.

When I got there I was taken into the office where I was faced with the school doctor. Her expression was shocked when she saw the state of me and she asked me to take a seat. She told me she'd noticed the bruises on Shane and that now, having seen the state I was in, had no doubt that Shane was at risk. I tried to assure her that I'd keep Shane safe and that it wouldn't happen again, but I knew she didn't believe me.

I returned home in a terrible panic, wondering where Shane and I could go. I didn't want to land on my auntie's doorstep again because I'd burdened her enough and I didn't have any friends I could turn to in the area. My mind was in turmoil, dreading the sound of Luke's key turning in the lock. I had to do something fast. But I couldn't think quickly enough: before I knew it three social workers had arrived to take Shane away.

'Mummy!' he screamed as they drove off in the car.

I ran after them, yelling my son's name and clutching my swollen stomach. The car drove around the corner and was gone. I slumped to the ground, sobbing uncontrollably. One of the social workers had stayed behind with me and helped me to my feet.

'You fucking bastards!' I cried, 'I want my son back!' I pushed the woman's hand off my arm, nearly losing my balance. She grabbed and steadied me.

'Come on,' she said. 'Let's get you checked out.'

'Shane,' I sobbed. 'I want Shane.'

'It's okay.' She helped me into her car and we headed for the hospital.

But I didn't care about myself; I'd lost the most important person in the world to me.

Chapter Ten

'Where's Shane?' I kept asking. 'I want to see my son!'

The pain of having Shane so forcefully taken away from me was so bad I felt as if I was about to give birth there and then and the nurse in the maternity wing of the local hospital was extremely concerned. Social workers and medical staff tried to calm me down, but I wasn't having any of it.

'Give me my son!'

The social workers were suspicious that I was the one to blame and however much I tried to persuade them that I loved Shane and wouldn't hurt him, that Luke was at fault and that I was a good mum they ignored me. I even begged the social workers to keep Shane until I could get away from Luke and find a safe place for the two of us to live, but it was plain that they viewed me as a child abuser. I sat in the hospital being prodded by doctors and nurses, swabbing my cuts and bruises, crying and mumbling that I'd never hurt my son.

In those days, being beaten black and blue and almost being strangled was classed as a mere domestic, so I wasn't kept in hospital for protection or driven to a safe house. The most I could do was take an injunction out against Luke and hope that would keep him away. Although I had the injunction I wasn't taking any risks and was too afraid to return to the house, so I went and stayed at Auntie's. My poor aunt and uncle; they were both in their sixties and I'd brought them enough trouble as it was. I was ashamed that I was dumping my problems on my family yet again.

'Don't be so daft, Cheryl,' Auntie and Uncle said when I apologised. 'You're family.'

I was allowed to have supervised visits with Shane, which was heartbreaking, especially when he held his arms out to me and sobbed 'Mummy, don't go!'

The social worker handling my case would look at me suspiciously and ask me why I hurt my son and tell me that if I admitted to my 'problem' she could find help for me. The social services wanted me to be guilty; they wanted to cast me in the evil mother role. I knew that they couldn't allow Shane to be put at risk, but surely they could see that I'd been beaten too? Surely they could see how much I loved my son?

If the situation wasn't awful enough, I had to go back to the house to get my belongings. Auntie Joyce and I were relieved to find that Luke wasn't lurking around. But our relief didn't last long and a few hours later he was banging on the door, asking to be let in and saying he wanted to pick up his things. Auntie and I looked at each other, wide-eyed, knowing exactly what my husband was capable of.

'Let me in, Cheryl.' Luke was rattling the letterbox. 'I need my clothes and stuff.'

I didn't know what to do for the best. The injunction meant he wasn't supposed to be anywhere near me, but I didn't want to tell him to go away and make his temper worse. He was likely to force his way into the house. I felt responsible for my auntie's safety so I decided the best course of action to take was to let him in and allow him to collect his clothes from the bedroom while Auntie and I stayed in the living room.

All seemed to be going well until he barged into the living room and flew at me screaming 'I hate you, you fucking bitch!' Then he hit me hard around the face, sending me flying.

'You leave her alone!' shouted Auntie, standing in front of me.

'Fuck off!' Luke walked over to her and smacked her around the face.

'Oh my God!' I screamed and ran to Auntie's side.

Auntie clutched her cheek and stood motionless, staring at Luke. I couldn't believe that even someone as evil as him would hit an elderly lady. We had no phone, so it wasn't as if I could call the police and I knew that Auntie wouldn't leave the house, even if I begged her to.

'Auntie, go upstairs.' I gently pushed her towards the living room door.

At first she refused, saying she was too scared to leave me, but I told her that I'd be okay and that Luke and I would sit down and discuss our situation calmly. I can still remember the look on her face as she turned to leave the room: sheer terror. My aunt had led a quiet life, busying herself with family and friends, and baking cakes. Violence was a million miles away from her world.

When she had gone upstairs I told Luke that we should talk about our marriage without getting angry, reminding him that we had our baby to think about. Immediately he lunged at me, hurling abuse and calling me disgusting names.

I dodged his grasp and headed for the back door, but

Luke grabbed me from behind and threw me to the floor with an almighty thud. I put my hands to my stomach to somehow protect my unborn child and begged Luke to think about what he was doing. He wasn't interested in listening, that was more than apparent. I tried to clamber to my feet, grasping onto one of the legs of the kitchen table, but Luke sighed and booted me back down.

'Get on the fucking floor where you belong, bitch!'

'Luke! Please!' I curled into the tightest ball I could and looked up into his face. A smirk spread across his lips as he slowly unzipped the flies of his jeans, pulled out his penis and urinated all over me.

'You're nothing but a fucking animal,' he said.

When he'd finished he shook the drops off his penis, tucked it back into his underpants and did his fly up. He took his foot off me and just stood there, grinning at me as I pulled myself to my feet with urine dripping from my hair.

I knew that if I didn't get away from him I was dead. I glanced towards the kitchen work surface, saw the biscuit tin, picked it up and smashed Luke around the head with it. The thing just ricocheted off his skull and clanged to the floor, breaking all the Rich Tea.

Luke laughed. 'I'm going to fucking kill you now,' he said.

For a few moments I thought that death would be a relief. I was so exhausted and humiliated I wanted to give up, but then I thought of Shane and my unborn child, and strength surged through my whole body. I screamed something and lunged at Luke, kicking him in the testicles. Then I grabbed a bread knife from off the sink drainer and pointed it at his stomach.

'I'll fucking kill you, you bastard,' I warned.

And God forgive me, I would have done. I admit it. I was going to thrust the knife into his body until he was dead. But as I raised the knife I felt my hand being held back by some unseen force. That knife wouldn't move a millimetre and nor would my hand. It was only later that I realised Ben was responsible for sparing Luke's life, as well as saving me from a prison sentence.

The police arrived, alerted by the neighbours, and Luke bolted from the house and jumped over the back fence.

Auntie came down from the bedroom and held me tightly, even though I was covered in urine, tears and snot. I repeated over and over how sorry I was for getting her involved in such a scene, and she told me not to be so silly, reassuring me that everything was going to be fine.

I was taken to hospital, Auntie went home and I found myself in a refuge for battered wives that had just opened.

The warden was called Molly, a great lady who didn't suffer fools gladly, and would wear multi-coloured tops and scarves that clashed outrageously. She was a good listener and spent hours counselling me, while I worked out how to regain custody of Shane.

I don't know why, but I decided to call my mum, perhaps to see if she could offer me some kind of support. I was feeling very lonely and vulnerable and hoped she might have mellowed since her outbursts over Ben's death.

'You've made your fucking bed so you can lay in it,' she said when I phoned her, and slammed the receiver down.

Wanting to hear a friendly voice, I rang Dad in Australia, who was now married. Poor Dad, the amount of times I called, but he never complained or judged and always listened, giving me the best advice he could. I even reversed the charges, which Dad accepted, and not once did I think about the cost or the strain I placed on his relationship with his wife. I must have driven them both to distraction with my tales of woe.

Before long, Mum and certain family members had started another campaign, spreading sick rumours about me battering Shane. Letters wishing my unborn baby and me dead began dropping on my auntie's doormat. I don't know how many she actually received because I'm sure she kept some of them from me.

Considering I had little trust in social workers I was in no mood to put up with another one, but I was introduced to someone called Dan, who was to deal with my case. After hearing my story he promised to help me get Shane back.

'Yeah, yeah. You bloody social workers; you're all the same. Full of crap,' I said.

But Dan never got annoyed with my negative attitude and he accepted the abuse I threw at him with good grace.

Eventually, after much persistence on Dan's part, I began to trust him and could see that he was genuinely concerned for Shane and me. It turned out he was also a single parent with a young son around Shane's age.

Dan became a great friend, and continues to be so to this day. I owe this kind and loyal man so much, although he always denies this.

'I was only doing my job, Cheryl,' he says.

Shane had been placed with foster parents, which I was angry and upset about, since I was more than capable of caring for him, but soon Dan arranged for me to have supervised visits with my son.

On the first visit, Dan took us to a lovely village pub with a playground for kids, so that I'd feel at ease and not watched over by social services.

But Shane's foster parents were there and I didn't like them on first sight, though they could have been Dr. Barnado and Mother Teresa and I'd have been suspicious – not to mention jealous. I'd been told that they were keen to adopt because, though they had a son a few years younger than Shane, they were unable to have any more kids of their own. This panicked me and I spoke to Dan about my concerns, and he constantly reassured me that Shane was going to come home to me sometime in the near future.

With Dan's help I kept in contact with Shane and was there for his first day of school, which also happened to be his fifth birthday. I felt a lump in my throat as I watched this tiny little boy disappear behind the school gates, all nervous and excited. I shed quite a few tears that day.

Christmas came and more tears were shed. I was allowed to take Shane's presents to him at his foster parents' home but I wasn't invited to stay for longer than an hour or so. I wanted to watch him play with all his new toys and enjoy Christmas lunch with him, and then sit around watching cartoons. It broke my heart saying goodbye and going back to the refuge without him.

I felt completely safe in the refuge, but when I went to town, I had to wear a disguise to avoid being recognised by

Luke. The social services might not have wanted me to have my son back, but they were good enough to lend me a wig, albeit a wiry one resembling a badly cut doll's hairdo. Here was I, six months pregnant, waddling down the street in a dodgy wig and dark glasses, constantly hiding behind cars and bushes and ducking into shop doorways.

Apart from the refuge there was one other place where I felt safe – the church. It was at the end of my road and I'd often wander in and sit in a pew to chat to God or think about Shane. I got to know the pastor and his wife quite well and trusted them enough to tell them what was going on and why I had to wear a lopsided wig. They were very kind and understanding, and we became good friends.

I continued to have supervised visits with Shane, and although each time I'd go back to the refuge in tears, I knew Dan was doing his utmost to get my case sorted out. We spent so much time together, planning our next move, that gossip about us became rife around both the town and throughout social services. We just ignored it, and Dan carried on spending much of his own spare time dealing with my case, even putting his job on the line for me. I told him that if all social workers like him there'd be more happy families in this world. Dan looked further than the professional or social point-of-view; he actually got to know the two of us, and that's why, when it was time to go to court to fight for Shane, I knew I had a true ally at my side.

Chapter Eleven

I had a compassionate barrister who was appalled at the way I'd been treated by social services. He told me he thought I was being held up as an example because there had recently been a big news story about social workers being lax in the case of a little girl who had been abused and murdered by her parents.

There was no way anyone was going to take Shane away from me and I told Dan and the barrister I was determined to get my son back. They promised their support too.

As I walked into court I felt almost a hundred feet tall: my strength and energy came rushing back and that old feeling, reminding me all would be okay in the end flooded through me. I just had to keep my faith and hope.

Auntie Joyce and Uncle Stan accompanied me to court and were as shocked and dismayed as I was to find out that Mum was in the building. We were even more shocked when my barrister told me that she hadn't come thousands of miles to stand by me, but was there to give evidence *against* me.

'The rotten cow,' I said.

Mum stood up in the dock in her best outfit, her hair styled neatly, and told everyone in the courtroom what a neglectful mother I was, that I didn't deserve my son and that I never washed Shane's nappies or fed him properly.

My barrister hated Mum on sight and was disgusted by her behaviour, so he really laid into her, bombarding her with questions and making her look as small as humanly possible as she stammered in the witness box. She didn't come out of that courtroom in a good light.

After deliberation, the judge decreed that I should be allowed to spend more time with Shane and that eventually I should be awarded full custody, providing I never went back to Luke. I promised the judge that Luke was no longer part of my life and that I'd be divorcing him as soon as possible.

I kissed and thanked all those that had stood by me and went back to the refuge, hoping I'd soon have my little boy by my side.

Although I was victorious, I knew I'd had a close call and had very nearly lost my child because of my abysmal taste in men. I'd put my son at risk and was willing to take responsibility for that, even though I'd never laid a finger on him myself. For this reason I'd say loudly and clearly to any woman finding herself in that situation: get out. Do anything you can think of. Go anywhere. Call the police, find your local refuge, go to your local church, hide, emigrate, or disappear off the face of the earth if you have to. Don't risk your life or your children's lives, don't take the violence, the humiliation, and most importantly of all, don't let anyone break your spirit. No one deserves that. Luke nearly broke mine and I cannot believe I let someone do all those terrible things to me. I didn't ask for the abuse, I know, but I didn't do enough to put a stop to it.

The guilt I feel over allowing Shane to go through all that still haunts me, especially when I found out years later that Luke had gone into his room one night and put a cigarette out on his arm. Shane was just five years old at the time.

This is something I will have to live with and I know Shane bears me no ill feeling over the incident, and we talk openly about the past. I just wish I could take some of that past back and give my son happier memories of his childhood. All I can do is carry on being the best mother I can be to him now.

At the time of the court case I'd had the feeling that something wasn't right about my pregnancy. I think after all the beatings I was worried about the health of the baby.

It was September 1981, and I was still in the refuge and had decided to go to church for bible study. As I lumbered out of the church I thought I felt my waters break so I got a cab and took myself off to the hospital. But it turned out that although I was in labour my waters hadn't actually broken, so the midwife carried out the procedure for me, hoping that it would speed things along.

For a second or so I felt sorry for myself, giving birth on my own when I could see other women around me surrounded by loving husbands and bunches of flowers, but I had little time for self-pity when I felt an awful pain, followed by a strong urge to push.

The midwife told me not to, saying that I wasn't dilated enough and that the time wasn't right. I screamed and screamed, telling the midwife and other staff that I could feel the baby's head coming.

'Don't be silly, dear,' the midwife said. 'It's not time.'

'It's on its way!' I screeched, agony stabbing my insides.

The midwife sighed as if to say that I was making a fuss about nothing and made her way to the door, followed by the nurse.

'I can feel the head! The baby's here!' I yelled as loudly as I could.

The midwife and nurse walked back towards me to see if what I was saying was true, and they were shocked to see that I was about to give birth. Minutes later I held a seven-pound baby boy in my arms.

But I noticed that he wasn't pink like most newborns; he was a dull, grey colour. I beckoned to the midwife to take a look, but she told me there was nothing wrong with him and that I was being paranoid. However much I repeated that I knew there was something gravely wrong with my child the more the midwife and nursing staff ignored me, going about their business and acting as if I didn't exist.

I knew that the hospital staff had read my case notes and were aware that I had a child in care, so they weren't prepared to treat me with the respect I deserved. Their judgemental attitude angered me and I vowed I wouldn't stop hassling them until they checked my son over properly.

My baby was taken to another room to be bathed and when he was given back to me by one of the nurses he was still a sickly bluish-grey colour. I was petrified and again asked one of the nurses to take a look at him, but for the umpteenth time they said 'There is absolutely nothing wrong with your baby!'

'Yes there is!' I answered. 'He shouldn't be this colour.'

And I was proven right; my child's breathing grew laboured, his colour got worse and an hour later he was rushed into intensive care and placed into an incubator, where he was given oxygen.

'Why didn't you bloody well listen to me hours ago!" I

bellowed at the staff. 'He could be dying because of your neglect! You think you know it all, don't you? Well you don't! I'm his mother and I knew he was ill. Look at the state of him!' I pointed a finger at the incubator where my tiny son fought for his life. 'You think I'm nothing, don't you? Well fuck you all!'

I was told to keep quiet and was pushed back to my bed, but it was soon announced that the baby's condition was critical and we were driven to Bristol Hospital in an ambulance so he could have further tests.

Tears flooded down my cheeks as I prayed and urged my son not to give up, to be strong. I whispered that Mummy loved him very much and that she'd always be there for him.

My prayers didn't seem to be working and on the way to Bristol the baby had one cardiac arrest after another. He was brought round each time, but the attacks made him weaker and weaker.

When we got to Bristol I was practically frogmarched into a room on my own. I was beside myself with worry and was desperate to be at my baby's side, yet the staff told me in no uncertain terms that I wasn't allowed to and that I had to go on a drip because I was still losing blood.

All I could hear were doctors and nurses rushing about, barking complicated medical terms. I asked several nurses what was going on and how my baby was, but no one would tell me anything. When I think about it, they didn't need to; I knew my son wasn't going to survive. I think I always had.

A doctor came into my room and told me that my baby

had some kind of lung disease that he'd never come across before, and that because my son had been given so much oxygen it had affected his brain. The doctor said that if he did live, he'd be a vegetable for the rest of his life.

'No!' I screamed. 'Not my baby!'

Left on my own again I broke down. Was it my fault? Had I killed my own child? If only I'd got away from Luke as soon as I found out I was pregnant. If only, if only, if only - the list was endless and futile.

While I lay sobbing, I heard a commotion outside my room and the loud voice of a man shouting swear words. There was no mistaking the gruff tone. It was Luke. Fighting off the medical staff, he barged his way into my room. The doctors and nurses had already been warned not to let him anywhere near me, but Luke had the strength of ten men when angry.

'You fucking bitch!' he spat in my face, yanking the drip out of my arm and sending blood spurting in all directions. 'Fucking die, you bitch!'

I had no energy to fight back and just lay there as the white sheets turned red. Then, just in time, he was grabbed by security and pulled out of the room, until the police turned up. They didn't do a very good job of subduing him because not long after Luke was screaming that he wanted to see his son and, fighting off the police, attacked the pastor who had come to visit me. Finally, the police took him away and arrested him.

After one of the nurses had patched me up, replaced my drip and changed the sheets I had a long talk with the pastor and he gave me words of comfort, telling me that if my son died he'd be in the hands of God and that I wasn't to worry. He told me he'd stay by my side throughout and I thanked him, glad of his strength and kindness.

Soon my baby had another cardiac arrest and I was taken to be with him. Just as I arrived at the nursery he had a further attack, so I outstretched my arms as if to say to the medical staff 'No more.' I couldn't bear to let such a frail body go through any more pain. I knew he was going to die and I thought it kinder to let him go peacefully.

My son passed away, but just seconds before he did he opened his eyes for the first time and looked at me, and I mean really *looked*. I'll cherish that moment forever. It was wonderful, truly wonderful.

My child was one week old when he died and I named him Shaun as I cradled him in my arms.

I stared down at Shaun, thanking God and asked him to take good care of my son. I told Shaun that Mummy loved him very much and would never forget him. I told him that God would look after him and that I'd see him again one day. The pastor put his hand on my shoulder and said a short prayer.

Auntie Joyce and Uncle Victor had turned up at the hospital and anguish showed on their faces as they watched me cuddle my son. Neither them nor the pastor said anything; there was nothing they could say.

Eventually a nurse came over and told me it was time she took Shaun away. His little body had grown cold, I'd been holding him so long, but I wasn't ready to hand him over.

'Just a bit longer,' I sniffed.

'Sorry, Mrs Parker,' the nurse said and tried to take

Shaun off me. I wasn't going to give up without a struggle and finally the nurse had to prise him out of my grasp. I cried, asking her to give him back as she disappeared out of the ward with my son covered in a tiny blanket. I was led back to my room by Auntie, Uncle and the pastor and was so distraught I let out a piercing, animal howl that must have been heard from one end of the hospital to the other. My family and the pastor tried their best to comfort me, but the agony was unbelievable and I slumped onto my bed, sobbing Shaun's name over and over.

I managed to calm down enough to ring Dad, who had been waiting by the phone, and give him the news. The line went silent and then his shaky voice said how sorry he was and that if there was anything he could do all I had to do was ask. I thanked him and told him how much I loved and missed him and he said the same to me. How I wished he were there to hold me in his arms and take some of the pain away. And how I wished I were a little girl again, sitting on my daddy's knee, playing with the big buttons on his tatty green cardigan.

I reassured Dad that I'd be okay and before I hung up I felt the urge to ask Dad to pass on a message to Mum, Lucy and all the others who had wished my baby dead that their wish had come true. I knew Dad wasn't vindictive enough to say such things to anyone, even though he considered their actions cruel. I just hoped that when they got the news they'd have the decency and humanity to feel guilty.

I decided I wanted Shaun cremated, but Luke, who was in police custody, said *his* son was to be buried. I didn't have the physical or mental strength to argue and I gave in.

At the funeral I carried Shaun's tiny white coffin into my local church, where the pastor was to hold the ceremony. The casket was so light I couldn't believe that my baby was really in there.

I placed the coffin at the front of the church with the pastor and took my seat next to my aunt, uncle and the warden Molly, who was sniffing into her handkerchief. We all cried floods of tears as the service went ahead.

Then, as we made our way to the graveside, me carrying Shaun's coffin, Luke turned up, handcuffed to a police officer.

'I'll kill you, you fucking bitch!' He screamed, struggling to free himself. 'You fucking whore!' echoed around the graveyard as Shaun was laid to rest. 'I'll beat your fucking head in!'

At that moment I wished I could give up and die, and go and join my son. I'd had just about enough of life.

Chapter Twelve

At last my divorce came through and, needing something to take my mind off Shaun's death, I concentrated on the church, attending services and helping out with community events.

Dan was always there behind me, reminding me that soon I'd have Shane with me permanently. His optimism rubbed off on me, giving me a little more faith in life and hope for a better future.

But soon Luke reared his ugly head again. He decided to attend the same church as I, bleating to the pastor, his wife and anyone else who'd listen that he was a changed man and that he wanted to become a born-again Christian – and even be baptised. I knew that he was up to something, but the pastor and his wife said that if I believed in God then I should forgive Luke and take him back; that forgiveness was the most important part of Christianity. They pointed passages out in the Bible, speaking of turning the other cheek and forgiving the sins of others.

I believed in God and forgiveness all right; I just didn't want to risk being killed or losing Shane for good. I told the pastor that there was no way on earth I would have anything to do with my ex. Hadn't I lost my precious baby because I'd been beaten when I was pregnant?

I tried as hard as could to persuade the pastor that Luke was acting, that he had a plan to get revenge, but he wouldn't listen and refused to believe what I was saying.

'Everyone deserves a second chance, Cheryl,' he said.

Even the local police had a good laugh when they heard that Luke had turned to the church. I was sorely disappointed that the pastor and his wife had taken Luke's side, considering they'd been through so much with me and we'd built up a close bond. It saddened me to acknowledge it, but it was time to cut ties with the pastor and his wife. I felt I couldn't trust them anymore, and I had Shane's and my welfare to consider. Luckily, the council offered me a two-bedroom flat in a town a few miles away. It meant a new beginning for my son and me.

The flat wasn't a palace, but I was beside myself with happiness when I moved in and went about decorating. I had hardly any money so I improvised, making curtains out of car rugs, borders out of wrapping paper and bedspreads out of dyed sheets, and painting pictures for the walls. The flat looked cosy and welcoming by the time I'd finished and I stood, hands on hips, surveying my artwork.

Eventually Shane was allowed to stay for a whole weekend with me, which was wonderful. We had such a great time, playing games, going to the park and reading bedtime stories. It was frustrating when I had to hand him back to his foster parents.

'I'm fed up of being patient, Dan,' I said. 'I'm fed up with everyone breathing down my neck, to see if I slip up.'

'Cheryl,' he said 'how many mothers get the chance to prove to other people that they are actually a good mother?'

Dan's words sounded odd at first and then I smiled, understanding what he was saying. His optimism proved right and after cutting through rolls of red tape, Shane came home. I collected him from his foster parents house and showed him his new room. I'd painted animals on the walls and collected as many toys as I could, even scouring second hand shops. He ran into the room and began playing at once, his face all flushed with excitement to be in his new house with his mum.

It snowed that Christmas and Shane dashed to the window, pointing and asking to go outside to play. We threw snowballs at each other and built a snowman, laughing and running about like maniacs. I picked Shane up and hugged and squeezed him so much he squirmed in my arms.

'Gerrof, Mummy,' he moaned. He was practically mothered to death, so pleased was I to have him back.

On Christmas morning I felt a small hand poke me awake. I opened my eyes to see Shane looking at me expectantly, asking if Santa had been yet. Bleary-eyed, I glanced at the clock. It had just gone four. I told Shane that Father Christmas was still busy delivering presents and to go back to bed for a while, which he did, but at six o'clock he was back in my room, dragging me out of bed. He couldn't wait to open his gifts that were under the tree.

I'd managed to gather enough money to buy Shane a few bits and pieces; a colouring set, pens, a few little cars and some sweets, which he was very pleased with. I didn't have anything to open, but I didn't care, I was just happy to be with Shane, watching cartoons and movies, eating Christmas dinner, and playing games. It was the best day I could remember for a long time.

Although I'd cut contact with the pastor and his wife, I kept in touch with a few of my friends from the church. I could pray at home, and realised that it was much more important to try and do your best for others, to be kind and to teach your child how to do likewise. Anyway, I wasn't about to return to the same church and be faced with Luke, so I kept myself to myself.

Not long after I was shocked to read the headline in the local paper 'Pastor Takes Knife to Fellow Church Member'. It turned out that the preacher's wife had been having an affair with a close friend of the couple's, and one of the pastor's congregation. The pastor had found out and gone round to the man's house to confront him. A fight had broken out, and the pastor had pulled a knife on his wife's lover and tried to stab him. After an arrest and court case, the pastor lost respect in the community, his job, wife and home.

Many times, the pastor and his wife had preached about family values and had tried to get me to go back to Luke.

'Being a Christian means you have to accept others' faults and mistakes. Turn the other cheek, Cheryl,' I'd been reminded.

'What a bloody cheek,' I thought as I read that article. I had no sympathy for either of them and thought what hypocrites they both were. I was glad to be out of it.

Shane had to go into hospital to have his tonsils out and while he was gone I had a call from Dan saying that Luke's probation officer had been in touch and Luke was claiming that I still had some of his belongings and he wanted to come to my flat to collect them.

FOR CRYING OUT LOUD

I didn't have any of Luke's stuff in my home and if I had found anything of his I'd have thrown it out at once. I told Dan this, but he said it would get Luke and the probation service off my back if I just let Luke and an officer come around to check. The probation officer had reasoned with Dan and said it might help Luke get over his fixation with the past and me if he could just come to the flat once.

In the end I agreed that he could check the place, as long as he was with his probation officer. Dan assured me that everything would be okay and that Luke would be kept a close eye on. I had deep misgivings about the situation, but hoped that once the visit was over I wouldn't be hassled by Luke any more.

I picked up Shane from hospital that evening and, along with Dan, we returned to the flat. At once, I sensed that something was wrong and when I switched on the light we were faced with a most hideous mess. Pink dye had been thrown all over the beige carpet, the glass on the top of the dining table had been smashed and plants had been thrown everywhere. Shane's favourite record, 'Dream Machine' by David Essex, had been stamped on, the kettle wire was cut, plates and cups were smashed and the contents of the fridge lay on the floor.

Shane was very upset about his record, which he'd driven me insane with, playing it ten times a day. He cried as he held the pieces in his hands, and I gave him a cuddle, promising him that I'd buy him the David Essex album when I could afford it.

Worse was to come: Luke had excreted all over my bed and urinated on the walls and floor of Shane's room.

I guess I just felt numb; nothing could surprise or shock me anymore. Dan, on the other hand, was furious that the probation officer had let Luke into my flat alone. He apologised, saying how guilty he felt for giving them my key, but he thought he'd been dealing with a trusted, fellow colleague and had no idea the man would be so irresponsible. I reassured Dan that he wasn't to blame and that Luke was a law unto himself.

He stormed off to his office to sort it all out and I cleaned the flat up, trying to make a joke out of it for Shane's benefit.

Dan returned with his son, Joshua, a bottle of Jack Daniel's and fish and chips. Sitting on the floor, we all ate and then the kids played, while Dan and I discussed the day's events. Dan told me he'd had stern words with the probation officer, who'd answered that Luke had pleaded with him to let him go alone so he could have time to come to terms with everything he'd done.

I decided to take the probation officer to court. It wasn't that I wanted compensation, so much as the principle. I was meant to be able to trust these people, to feel protected, and they'd given a madman my front door key, so he could do whatever he liked in my own home. The probation service needed to be shown that it wasn't acceptable to leave people in such a vulnerable predicament.

It went to court and I represented myself, not that had any idea what I was doing. I just stood up, told the truth and that was that. The probation service couldn't deny anything because Dan had seen what had happened, and it was obvious that the officer shouldn't have left a man with Luke's record to his own devices. I was awarded sixty pounds in compensation. It was a pathetic amount, but at least I felt that justice had been done.

Days after the court case there was a long ring on the doorbell. I wasn't expecting anyone and never answered the door unless a friend phoned me first. It had to be Luke.

The bell rang again and again, so I shouted that I was in the bath and would be out in a moment. This stalled my unwanted visitor enough for me to call the police. I shook with fear and bundled Shane into the bathroom, ordering him to lock the door behind him. The poor mite looked up at me with bewilderment on his face, but I didn't have time to come up with a story fit for a child's ears. I had to act quickly.

With Shane safe in the bathroom I dashed to the kitchen, grabbed the biggest, sharpest kitchen knife I could find and ran to the top of the stairs, praying the police would turn up before anything terrible happened.

The glass pane in the front door was smashed inwards and I could see Luke's hand reaching through, trying to unlatch the lock. I held the knife out in front of me with both hands. I could feel my heart beating wildly against my chest and I could hardly catch my breath. Luke's fingers were picking the last chunk of glass out of the front door as the sirens sounded. Relief swept through me and I dropped the knife to my side.

Luke ran through the back garden and over the fence, disappearing into the distance.

'You silly bastards!' I shouted when the police turned up. 'Why did you have to advertise that you were on your way? Why didn't you just get a fucking brass band to announce your arrival? Now he's got away.'

But did they care that they'd lost Luke and hadn't caught him breaking his injunction? No. They had other issues on their minds.

'What's that in your hand?' asked a policeman, pointing at the nine-inch blade I was trying to hide behind my back.

'I was making sandwiches,' I said.

'I don't think that's true, is it?' his colleague was frowning.

Of course it wasn't true. I'd have brandished a bloody machine gun if it meant keeping Luke at arm's length.

After a few more questions, the police left and I collected Shane from the bathroom, telling him that a nice policeman had come to visit. He seemed undaunted and went to his room to play with his crayons and colouring books.

Events had been so hectic that I hadn't even had time to grieve properly for Shaun, although I thought of him often. I knew he was in a better place and heaven knows what his life would have been like with Luke as a father. I still felt guilt over his death, but I knew I had to keep things on an even keel for Shane.

Our life was quiet for once. Shane liked his new school and I'd made some good friends. The peace wasn't to last though.

I was having a cup of tea at my friend Anne's house while Shane was at school when there was a loud bang on the door. We both jumped out of our seats. I'd met Anne at the refuge and was so happy when I found out she was moving close to me. Her husband had been violent too and the council had re-housed her and her three kids. As soon as she heard the banging she was sure her husband had found her and was coming to beat her up again. I went to the door to try and reason with him, but it wasn't Anne's husband. It was Luke.

I opened my mouth to say something, but I was so shocked nothing came to mind. I began to shake and back away from him, trying to make my mind work, but it wouldn't.

Luke called me several filthy names, grabbed me by the hair and started dragging me screaming towards my flat. Anne followed us outside, throwing insults at Luke in her loud voice and telling him to leave me alone. Anne shouted at me not to worry, that she'd soon have the police around. Luke told her if he heard any sign of a police siren he'd kill me. I assured Anne that I'd be okay and that she was to go home and not tell anyone what was going on.

Once we were inside the flat, Luke threw me on the sofa and ordered me to listen to what he had to say. I kept my head down, staring at my hands and because I wouldn't look at him as he began to speak he punched me in the mouth. Blood dripped into my lap.

'You're a fucking murderess,' he said. 'You killed Ben and now you're trying to kill me, aren't you?'

I nodded, hoping that if I agreed with him he wouldn't hit me any more.

'You're nothing but a whore, aren't you, Cheryl? Go on, what are you? Huh? You're a whore. Go on.' Luke poked me. 'What are you?'

'A whore,' I repeated.

'You killed Ben, didn't you? Huh? What did you do, Cheryl?' Another poke.

'I killed Ben. I killed Ben,' I said.

Luke made me repeat time and time again that I was a worthless whore and that I'd killed Ben and was trying to kill him. This went on for what seemed like hours, then, all of a sudden, he stood up, went to the kitchen and made himself a cup of tea. He came back into the living room and said what a mess I'd got myself into, telling me that I should clean my face.

I went to the bathroom, looked in the mirror and knew that that was it. If I didn't get out of the flat this time I was going to die. Luke had lost it. He never stayed calm for long and I didn't know how to deal with him next.

So I did the only thing I could think of. I got down on my knees in front of the toilet, closed my eyes tightly and prayed as hard as I could. I prayed for strength. I prayed for guidance. I asked God for his help. I cried out for courage with every part of my body and soul. This was my very last chance.

When I opened my eyes I saw that the room had filled with a bright, white light – like the one I saw back in Adelaide when Ben was asleep beside me. With the light a feeling of calm and knowledge flooded through me, reassuring me that I would be safe. I stopped shaking, my fear dissolved and strength surged through my body. I got to my feet, cleaned my face and went back into the living room, where Luke was waiting for me.

I sat on the sofa opposite him and said nothing. Once again, Luke began to yell terrible accusations and lies at me, but I didn't care and I wasn't particularly scared. Whatever he said I was or had done, I agreed.

'Yes, Luke, I am a fucking whore,' I repeated. 'I'm a fucking murderess and I deserve to die.'

I told him it was my fault that he'd acted in the way he had over the past months. I begged him to forgive me for being such an evil whore and I cried and grovelled. It was the best performance of my entire life. In fact, I was performing to *save* my life. It worked. Luke had had enough for the time being. He stood up and left.

I stood up too. Then I dropped to my knees, and with tears flooding down my face, I thanked God for saving me.

Seeing that he'd gone, Anne came rushing in to see if I was okay and then phoned Dan, who said he'd pick Shane up from school for me and take us both to a friend's place for a few days. I was pleased to get away for a while, but I wondered how long it would be until Luke returned.

Chapter Thirteen

I was well and truly off men, but I had a very persistent friend who said she knew this guy who was perfect for me. You know what it's like when you're the only single person, surrounded by couples; they're desperate to set you up so you fit in or you don't try and steal their partner. Anyway, I agreed and was introduced to Tom.

He was a local man: tall, dark and reasonably good-looking, with a steady job in computing. It turned out that many of the other women in the village saw him as a bit of a catch, especially given that most of the other single men around were on the dole.

I liked Tom straightaway and we found we had lots to talk about. One date turned into several and soon we were virtually inseparable. Tom took me out several nights a week – mainly to his favourite pub, where he was a member of the darts team. He introduced me to all his friends there, who seemed like a nice crowd.

Tom made a real fuss of Shane too, buying him toys, clothes and even a TV for his room. In fact, he spent a lot of money on both of us, buying new furniture, kitchen equipment and a TV for the flat, as well as clothes and jewellery for me. I didn't ask or expect him to do so, but I was very grateful since I was on benefit and completely broke. After Luke, it made a welcome change to be cared for and spoilt.

I introduced Tom to Dan and a few days later Dan told me he wasn't keen on my new boyfriend and had a bad feeling about him. When I asked him why, he couldn't explain it and said it was a gut reaction. He said he'd have Tom checked out to see if he had a record, reminding me that Shane was still on the at-risk register and that I couldn't afford to get involved with another unsavoury character. I agreed and told Dan to see what he could come up with, hoping that Tom didn't have a shady past, which would mean I'd have to stop seeing him.

The results came back squeaky clean. I was relieved because I was falling for Tom and he seemed to feel the same way about me.

One day Tom told me he had a surprise for me. He said he thought it was time I had a car of my own, nothing fancy, and had arranged for us to pick one up that evening. He still wouldn't tell me what type of car it was.

'You'll see when we get there,' he grinned.

It was a blue Mini and I fell in love with it at once, naming it 'Humpty'. I got my British licence and spent hours driving around with the widows wound down and music blaring, thinking how wonderful life was: Shane was happy, I had a great boyfriend and a nice home; and I had just landed a new job as a sales assistant for a shoe repair company. I was proud that I was now a respectable member of society and had put my past mistakes behind me.

After a few months, Tom introduced me to his mum, who I got on well with straightaway. She absolutely adored Shane, treating him like her own grandson and plying him with sweets and fizzy pop.

Not having a daughter, Tom's mum was pleased to have me around and made a fuss of me, no doubt glad of some female company. However, Tom wasn't particularly close to her, and I think he only visited her out of duty; he didn't seem to bother much with his two brothers either. I guessed that his Mum had been quite strict with them all as they grew up and that perhaps Tom resented her for that. I did wonder why he was so distant with his brothers, but I didn't want to ask questions; he was good to Shane and me, so that was all that mattered as far as I was concerned. I'd had quite enough of family secrets and dysfunctional pasts, and I was keen not to go down that route again.

Tom was always telling me how much he loved me and how great it was to be with me. I lapped up the attention and was proud to be seen on the arm of the biggest catch in the village. I often saw the other girls in the neighbourhood throwing me jealous glances and I'd carry on smiling, holding Tom's hand tight. We were so much in love and I was happier than I could remember.

Within a year of our getting together, Tom and I bought our first home. It was such fun choosing new furniture for the place, browsing around department stores, looking at soft furnishings and making our home as cosy as possible. Along with the TV in Shane's room, he had a video and stereo. I didn't want to spoil him, but he'd been through so much because of me that I thought it was time that he enjoyed himself.

Tom was earning a lot of money and with my income we had everything we could wish for. I thought back to the days when Shane and I were in that awful hotel and had to tramp the streets all day, sitting on park benches or window-shopping. I thought too of the tiny flat that Luke had trashed. How different our lives were now.

Tom was working very long hours and when he did have free time he spent it playing darts, cricket or football. Our house was ruled by sport and it was always on the TV. It got on my nerves at times, but I didn't say anything, reasoning that Tom deserved his hobbies and that they helped him to wind down after working so hard for the three of us.

Soon Tom and I discussed having a child of our own and as I was adamant that I wouldn't have a child out of wedlock, we decided to set a date for our wedding.

When I told my family I was to be married, I was greeted with comments like 'Let's hope this one lasts' and 'Try and make it work this time.' I couldn't blame them for saying such things, with my track record. I assured them that Tom was different: kind and loving and good to my son. My aunt and uncle seemed to like Tom, which I was relieved about.

Tom and I had a small wedding in the church near our home in Gloucestershire. Uncle Victor gave me away and the rest of our guests consisted of Auntie Joyce, my other aunt and uncle and Tom's mum, dad and brothers, plus a few friends. Shane was there too and he beamed at me, all smart in his new shirt and trousers.

I was disappointed that our honeymoon was only a weekend in Wales, but Tom had work commitments so we had to make do. Tom said he could understand my disappointment and that we could go on holiday at a later date, when his job was less time-consuming. I shrugged and agreed. A flash honeymoon didn't make a marriage, after all; it was the relationship that mattered.

The following weekend Dan made up for it by taking Shane, his son Joshua and I canoeing, something Shane and I hadn't done before and we were both excited at the prospect.

The weather was gloriously sunny, perfect for a day on the river, and as we lowered the canoe into the water I warned Dan to be careful it didn't capsize. Dan scoffed in a confident manner and assured me that such a thing had never happened to him before and it wasn't likely to either. Shane, Joshua and I climbed in to the wobbly canoe, while Dan tried to steady it and then when he went to step in the whole thing overturned, throwing us all in to the water with a great splash. The boys panicked at first, until we realised that the river wasn't very deep, and we clambered up onto the bank, laughing and shrieking. We laughed even harder when we noticed that there was one person missing. Dan's false leg had got stuck in the mud and he couldn't move an inch. He pulled, but it still wouldn't budge. In the end Dan had to unfasten his false leg and the rest of us helped him hobble to land, before I went back into the muddy water to retrieve the rest of his leg. The four of us had tears of laughter pouring down our faces and poor Dan was so embarrassed, especially when we returned to my house with his leg making loud farting sounds as he walked.

Dan took a shower while I cleaned his leg, and I wasn't surprised to find out that I was the cause of gossip in the area for the weeks following. It was a small village and everyone knew everyone else's business, but if I'd waited for Tom to take us out for a day in the country I'd have been waiting a very long time. He spent most of his days at work or enjoying his sporting hobbies. I wished he could be with me more, but then I told myself not to be so ungrateful. At least he wasn't lazy or abusive.

Shortly after our wedding I came home to find that a ripped-up photo of Shane and me had been posted through the letterbox. I showed it to Tom and told him that Luke was on the warpath again, but he didn't seem at all bothered.

'Please don't go out tonight, Tom. I'm scared he'll come back,' I said.

'I'm not having your ex controlling what I do and where I go,' he answered.

I tried to make Tom see sense, reminding him how dangerous Luke was and what he was capable of doing, but he shrugged and went to his darts match, leaving Shane and me alone.

I slumped onto the sofa; my fear mixed with disappointment. If Tom loved and cared for me he should have been by my side and made sure that Luke stayed away, not gone to the pub with the boys. At that moment I realised that our marriage wasn't quite what I'd hoped for and that we had a few issues to tackle.

Luke didn't return that night, but when I was driving to work the next day the steering went out of control, sending me careering all over the road. When I managed to stop I found that the wheel nuts on my car had been loosened.

'Bastard!' I shouted. 'Why can't you leave me alone?'

I reported the incident to the police, who checked for the car for fingerprints, then went to Luke's home and arrested him. I'm not sure what happened in court and I didn't want to know; I'd had enough of Luke to last me several lifetimes. But whatever happened it was enough to warn Luke off and he left me alone. Eventually I realised that he'd given up stalking me and I began to relax. He was actually out of my life for good.

It was just as well he was because I had enough to deal with at home. After six months of trying for a baby, I found out I was pregnant and was thrilled. Tom was pleased too, that is until it became time for me to give up work. Perhaps it was the strain of having to provide for his family from his wage alone, but he started getting short-tempered and would sometimes snap at me.

Once I asked Tom if he would spend more evenings at home, now that I had stopped work and didn't have much social interaction.

'Don't be such a selfish bitch, Cheryl! Who d'you think fucking pays for all this?' he snarled, waving his hand about the room. 'I fucking do and if I want to go out and enjoy myself every night I bloody well will, so shut up!'

I couldn't believe what I was hearing. Tom had never insulted me like that before. He wasn't happy picking on just me, and turned his attention to Shane, shouting at him if he didn't do what he was told immediately or if his chores weren't finished on time. Poor Shane physically shrank when Tom walked into the room.

'Oh, God,' I thought. 'Not again.'

I was soon making excuses for Tom's behaviour, persuading myself that it was the pressure of his job and that once the baby was here he'd cheer up and go back to normal. In the back of my mind though the warning bells were ringing themselves silly.

I was four months pregnant when events took a turn for the worse. Tom and I were in the middle of a row – probably about money or his sport – when I swore at him and he whacked me around the face. It stung badly, but my first instinct was to hit him back, which I did, and then I ran before he could do it again.

I tried to forget about the incident and relative calm returned to the house. A few weeks later, however, Tom started calling me horrible names and almost pushed me over for not getting out of the way of the television fast enough. He'd didn't want to miss one moment of his precious cricket.

It was obvious that the abuse was starting all over again and I know now that I should have taken Shane and got out of the house after that first slap, but like many other women in such situations I told myself to try and keep the peace. I thought that if I did what Tom wanted he wouldn't lose his temper and there would be no more hitting or pushing. That would be an end to it.

It may seem ridiculous to those who haven't been in abusive relationships and many people have asked me why I got myself into such a mess and why I put up with it. Before I got involved with Luke I used to think the same about women in violent marriages or relationships. I thought that they were mad or pathetic for letting a man hit them.

My only explanation is that with every abusive episode the fear grows, until gradually it takes over every minute of every day, of every week. This man who shares your home, your bed and your life knocks any shred of self-esteem out of you with his sneers, his insults and his fists. It's silly I know, but even after all this you still don't want to admit defeat, so you cling on to the hope that this man you once loved, who loved you, might change. You fantasise that you'll wake up one morning and he'll be there with breakfast in bed and a big bunch of flowers and that he'll shower you with loving hugs and kisses. He'll be a changed man. But he never does change. Any man who is willing to hit a woman, to beat her physically, insult her and break her mentally will never change.

Having gone through what I had with Luke, I was pretty sure that it was only a matter of time before I'd have to end my marriage to Tom. I simply couldn't take it again. But I was pregnant and had to choose my moment carefully. If someone had come along and offered me a place to live I'd have gone right there and then, yet it doesn't work like that. I was on my own, and afraid of taking such a big step.

In September 1984 Lee was born by emergency caesarean and weighed in at seven pounds. At first I was too scared to look at him, in case he was that awful grey colour that Shaun had been, but Lee was pink and healthy and I cried with relief when I held him in my arms.

Tom was proud to be a father and seemed to soften his attitude towards me when I was in the hospital, only when we took the baby home his mood was worse than before and Shane bore the brunt of his foul temper. Tom was forever shouting at Shane to keep quiet and not wake his little brother up, and he'd send him to his room if Shane so much as asked for a biscuit in a voice Tom thought was too loud. If Tom ordered Shane to do a chore or collect something from the kitchen for him and Shane didn't run quick enough, there was havoc.

'Move it!' he'd bellow.

Evenings were a nightmare, because Tom would demand to see what Shane's teachers had set him for homework and if Shane took too long to finish it he'd get a terrible telling off.

'Hurry up, get on with it! Go on, stupid!' Tom would rant. 'Honestly, Cheryl, you've got a right dunce here.'

'Stop calling Shane names. He's got a name,' I'd say.

I pleaded with Tom to leave Shane alone, reminding him that my son was just eight years old.

Tom would sneer and say 'Shut up, woman. You don't know what you're talking about. The boy needs discipline. You've spoilt him!'

I was so grateful when Tom landed a contract that meant he had to work away during the week, leaving the three of us to ourselves. Shane was more relaxed and regained his old confidence now that he could play be a boisterous kid again.

Lee was a good baby, sleeping right through the night, feeding well and sitting in his high chair gurgling away, but I thought it would do me good to get out of the house for a few hours and also bring in some money of my own. I had a feeling that there would soon come a time when I'd need to have a little cash behind me, and I was sick of relying on Tom, who loved to remind me what a financial burden Shane and I were.

I got a part-time job looking after the elderly in a residential home near where we lived and Tom's mum was more than pleased to have Lee with her.

While the weekdays were bliss for the three of us, I grew to hate the weekends when Tom came home. He'd sit in his favourite chair with the football loud on the TV, shouting 'Yes!' whenever a goal was scored and springing out of his chair with excitement, his fist punching the air. Even though the noise from the TV was deafening, he'd pick on Shane, barking 'Shut your noise, I'm trying to watch the game!'

He expected Shane and me to wait on him hand and foot and wouldn't lift a finger in the house for himself, Lee or anyone. I can't remember a time when he buttered a slice of toast or took his glass out to the kitchen. I'm surprised he didn't order me to go to the toilet for him, so loath was he to move out of his chair. Quite often I'd stand behind that damn chair, with the shouting of the crowds blasting from the TV and think about how wonderful it would be to clock Tom over the back of the head with a saucepan.

'I work hard all week. I'm entitled to a rest,' Tom would reply when I complained about him loafing about.

'But you hardly ever see Lee,' I reminded him.

'I've bloody well seen him, woman, so stop your nagging. I can't hear the telly!'

'I'd like to shove that fucking telly up your arse,' I'd mutter on the way to the kitchen to make dinner.

When he wasn't watching sport he was playing darts in the local pub or enjoying a game of cricket or football. When he did show an interest in his son he expected me to be impressed by his efforts. It was as if he was doing his family a favour just by being in the house. I wasn't bothered if he stayed away for good; I was just annoyed that he neglected Lee, especially as he'd been so enthusiastic for us to have a child of our own.

Tom's utter selfishness carried on into the bedroom and he'd demand sex as if it was his right to have it when and how he wanted. I'd gone off the idea, but Tom hadn't and wasn't interested in excuses. I'd lay there with him grunting like an warthog on top of me, trying to take my mind of what was happening by thinking about what I was going to cook for dinner the next day or about something I'd read about in the paper.

Once Tom had finished he'd turn his back to me and, within minutes, the room echoed with his loud snores that reminded me of an emptying waste disposal.

After years of being married to Tom I'd lay in bed staring at his back and silently ask myself, 'Cheryl, why do you attract such crap men, you silly, *silly* cow?'

If I'd a pound for every time this question came into my head I'd have had enough money to retire by the age of thirty-three.

Chapter Fourteen

I was speechless when Auntie Joyce phoned to tell me that Lucy had rung her, wanting to get in touch with me again. I hadn't spoken to my sister since Ben died, and the last contact she'd made with me was when my mother and her had sent me poisonous letters saying that I wasn't a fit mother and they wished my baby dead.

Lucy told my aunt that she felt bad and that she had misjudged me over the years and wanted us to get together and sort everything out. She'd moved back to England a year or so earlier and offered to get the train to Gloucestershire.

Initially I was annoyed and didn't see why I should have to meet her and justify myself to someone who was meant to be on my side, instead of making my life a misery by being so vindictive. She hadn't taken the time to ask me how I truly felt about Ben's suicide or why Shane had been taken into care. She'd automatically sided with Mum and assumed the worst of her own sister.

I thought long and hard about Lucy's attempt at reconciliation and, in the end, decided that I should meet her. We'd been close once and I was curious to see if there was a possibility that we could go back to the way we'd been when we were younger. If she was willing to admit her mistakes and listen to my side of the story, then I would be very happy to have my big sister back in my life. I'd missed her a lot. I was in constant touch with Sheena and I hoped that the three of us could enjoy a proper sisterly relationship. Both had helped bring me up and it would have been such a shame if we'd cut ties altogether. As the days went by the more I thought about seeing Lucy again and the more excited and anxious I grew.

Lucy came a month later and as I waited at the train station to pick her up my stomach fluttered. I wondered how we'd get on and if we'd even recognise each other; it had been so long since we'd been face to face. But as Lucy stepped off the train I spotted her at once and we locked eyes, smiled and ran towards each other for a hug and kiss. We made our way home and talked about old times and all that had happened since we'd last met.

Lucy brought up Ben's death and explained that she had thought I was to blame at the time; that's why she'd agreed with Mum and sent the letters. She admitted that the letters were absolutely awful and that she shouldn't have sent them, but she'd been very angry, thinking my behaviour was irresponsible and selfish. I told her how unhappy I'd been with Ben and that I hadn't meant for him to end up so distraught that he'd taken his own life. I talked of the deep guilt I'd felt. I also showed her newspaper clippings about Luke and his crimes and she was very shocked, not to mention embarrassed that she'd posted letters accusing me of being an abusive mother and saying that she wished my baby would die. We discussed Shaun's death and tears welled in Lucy's eyes as my story unfolded. She shook her head, unable to take it all in.

'I'm so sorry I misjudged you,' she said, and gave me a cuddle.

'It's okay, Lucy,' I said, glad that we were friends again. I didn't dare tell her that I'd entered into yet another unhappy relationship. She'd probably have told me how stupid I was and got on the first train back to her home and family in London.

Lucy spent the weekend with us and I was glad to see that Tom was on his best behaviour, when he wasn't in the pub throwing darts. He was polite to my sister and stopped picking on Shane in her presence, but he didn't go out of his way to be friendly and Lucy was the same.

Eventually the subject of Mum came up, and Lucy asked me if I'd see her. She told me that The Lad had left Mum and that she was lonely and missed her family. Mum had also moved back to England and had a place in south London, worryingly close to Sheena. Sheena still wanted nothing to do with our mother and I guessed that Mum was scared she'd lost me permanently as well.

The thought of meeting her again sent shivers through me and I fretted over whether I should go ahead with Lucy's suggestion. Mum had let me down badly with her spitefulness, and I was so very angry with her over her being a witness against me in court. I didn't ask Tom for his opinion because all he'd have said was 'It's up to you.'

For days I pondered, paced and mulled the situation over in my mind. Could I face Mum? How would I feel when I saw her? Wasn't forgiveness the best option? In the end I decided that I'd meet her and I told Lucy so. Lucy was really pleased and arranged for us to go to Mum's house.

I was surprised when Tom offered to drive Shane, Lee and me to London for the reunion, considering there was probably a cricket match on the TV, and I thanked him for his consideration. Perhaps our relationship was improving after all.

Thoughts of my marriage faded into the background as we neared London and I realised that although I wasn't really looking forward to seeing Mum, I wasn't remotely nervous either. I felt kind of indifferent and knew that if she started with her accusations and awkward behaviour I'd just leave. There was no way I'd let her hurt me again. I'd had enough.

But surprisingly, Mum was charming and made us very welcome. She hadn't changed at all since I'd last seen her and looked slim and healthy, and she giggled as she fussed over the boys.

'Isn't Lee just *gorgeous*?' she cooed, brushing her hand over the baby's cheek. It was the first time she'd seen her grandson, who was now eighteen months old, and it seemed she was smitten with him.

I deliberately kept away from talk of the past and waited to see if Mum would bring the subject up. And she did, just as we were about to leave.

She put her arms around me. 'I'm so sorry. I was wrong,' she said and began to cry.

I couldn't believe that she had actually apologised and seemed to mean it. She didn't try to excuse what she'd done either, which made her admission of guilt all the more surprising and believable.

As the weeks passed I spoke to Mum on the phone several times and I decided to let go of my bad memories and not let blame and recriminations get in the way of our renewed friendship. Mum had made mistakes, but so had I, and I was quite aware, as I am now, that nothing good ever came from harbouring bitterness or bearing a grudge.

Eventually Mum and I got to the point where we were able to talk frankly with one another, while acknowledging that we had different outlooks on life and would have to agree to disagree at times. This decision suited us both well.

I had become dreadfully unhappy living in such a small village and told Tom that I wanted to move to an area where there were more people and a bit more going on. I couldn't stand the way that everyone knew everyone else's business and gossiped about one another.

Much to my surprise, Tom agreed and suggested that we sell up and move to a town in West Sussex, near where he worked. I liked the idea and we rented a place there, intending to buy a house when we returned from Australia, where we were to visit my dad. Once again, Tom was on his best behaviour while we were in Adelaide, though much of the reason he was so charming was that he'd made sure our visit coincided with a major cricket tournament out there. The boys and I spent all our time with Dad and his wife and Tom enjoyed most of his days sitting in a cricket pavilion or watching the tournament on TV. Dad couldn't believe that he'd come all this way to watch cricket. However, it was fantastic to be with Dad, so I wasn't overly disappointed that Tom wasn't around much, and I think Dad was too busy lavishing his attention on Lee and Shane to notice that my husband and I weren't exactly the closest of couples.

I was sad to leave Dad, but we had to return to England and house hunt. We found a detached house in West Sussex and even Mum pitched in with the move, packing boxes and heaving furniture about, as we worked hard to make the new house look its best. I wanted everything to be in place by the time Tom got home from work, so we spent hours putting curtains up, hanging pictures, hiding toys and clothes in cupboards and making sure that everything was in place. By the time we'd finished you'd have thought we'd been living there for weeks.

I put the boys to bed and Mum and I slumped on the sofa, sipping wine, relieved to have the chance to relax. We surveyed our surroundings and clinked glasses.

'Phew, I'm knackered,' said Mum.

At that moment Tom walked into the house, mumbled 'hello', went upstairs and then came back down again, demanding to know where his favourite toothbrush was.

'You useless bastard!' shouted Mum. 'You walk in here that big head of yours and ask where your fucking toothbrush is! What about the house? You don't bat a fucking eyelid!' Mum was shaking her finger at Tom, who towered above her. 'Why the fuck Cheryl married you, I'll never know!'

Tom just looked down at my mother with a nonchalant expression, sniffed and went back upstairs.

'Yeah, go on!' she shrieked after him. 'Piss off, you useless prat!'

For once I had to agree with her.

'Your taste in men hasn't improved, Cheryl. He's a right loser,' she said.

I shrugged. Mum was good at stating the obvious.

Tom and I drifted further and further apart. I was

working full time for a travel company, as well as looking after the kids and house. Tom said that because he was bringing in so much money he didn't see why he should have to do chores or even take the kids to school or nursery, and he still spent his spare time with his nose pressed to the sports programmes on TV or in the pub.

I made sure that the children didn't lose out though, and we'd play football in the park, go for picnics or visit my dad's side of the family as often as possible. If Tom wasn't interested in us I was going to ensure our lives were as normal as I could. He was the one who was missing out.

Tom's complete indifference towards me also spurred me on to pursue an ambition I'd had since I was a child: music. A woman at work told me about her boyfriend and how he'd just finished recording a track. She played me his demo and I liked it very much, and I was soon dying to get in the studio myself. I was thirty-two and quite aware that people in the industry would consider me too old for pop star material, but I was determined to give it a go.

With my kind colleague's contacts I wrote and recorded a song and after a few more practice sessions left the studio with my very first professional demo tape, co-written with a well-known man in the record business and entitled 'Go On, Girl'. I was so happy when I took that tape home and listened to it a hundred times, hoping that my music hobby could somehow turn into a career. I'd found something I really loved and was determined to carry on, so I did my best to try and sell the song to several companies, only I didn't have a manager or professional backing and no one took me seriously. I was disappointed but I wasn't giving up.

Tom was disdainful of my newfound ambitions and would make comments like 'I don't know why you're wasting your energy on all that rubbish. You're past it.' He resented the time I spent away from the house and wasn't pleased that I was making new friends with whom I found I had much in common.

Thoroughly fed up with his uncaring attitude, I decided that I couldn't bear sharing a bedroom with him anymore and moved my clothes and belongings into the spare room.

Tom was shocked when I announced that I wanted us to consider my actions as a separation.

'But all marriages are like this,' he said.

'Well you can stick your fucking marriage then,' I said. 'I've had enough.' I threw one of his precious cricket jumpers in his face and went off with a pile of my own clothes. I was only travelling as far as the other side of the wall, but it was a start.

Chapter Fifteen

Tom's ego was severely dented and he started to act even more strangely, insisting that I pay rent for the spare room, on the basis that I was now his lodger. I couldn't be bothered to argue and just did as he asked.

'Tom, would you mind getting out of my room please?' I said on several occasions, when I'd look up from the book I was reading or the pad I was scribbling song lyrics on and catch him scowling in the doorway. He would stare at me with such hatred, and I grew more uncomfortable as the days went by. The sooner I was able to move out with the children the better. Something – or someone - was constantly telling me that Tom was about to really lose his temper and I didn't want to be around to witness it. I was sure it wasn't just woman's intuition; the warning was more tangible than that.

I told my mum about of my fears and although she agreed wholeheartedly that I should end my marriage, she assured me that she couldn't imagine him doing anything drastic. I wished I had the same faith. I should have left Tom the first time he hit me, but I'd hung around, hoping for a miracle. I must have been delusional - or just plain daft. I'd gone through untold misery with Luke and here I was, sharing a home with another bad tempered bloke. I still kick myself for my stupidity and others say 'What on earth were you thinking of?'

'Don't ask me,' I answer, more than a little embarrassed.

I tried hard to ignore my worries and concentrate on my

music so I wrote a new song called 'Passion'. I was extremely nervous about the recording session and took Mum along for moral support, but my jitters got the better of me and I kept messing up one particular word. I can't remember what the word was, but it wasn't a particularly long or complicated one and I felt like a moron, standing there, stuttering. I could see the producer, engineer, the backing singers and Mum peering at me from the other side of the studio and my panic rose, making me stumble all the more. In the end the producer came up to me with a huge tumbler full of brandy and told me the alcohol would relax me. Mum wasn't pleased and said 'Excuse me, my daughter does not drink!'

'She bloody does now,' I said, and snatched the brandy, gulped it down and got on with the song, feeling wonderfully confident. But by the time I reached the very last note I fell on the floor, headphones and all. Mum got me a glass of water and eventually I sobered up.

The music producer and even Mum were very enthusiastic about the end result and I was surprised at how sexy my voice sounded, thanks to the producer's coaxing. How I hoped that 'Passion' would be a big success and that some record executive would snap it up. I sent my demo out to music publishing companies and other people in the business and waited for a response.

Meanwhile, Tom's behaviour towards me was getting worse and he'd demand to know where I was going or who I was going to meet. He was fine with Lee – when he bothered to spend time with him – but he'd shout at Shane and call him names. I couldn't stand the atmosphere any longer and knew it was a matter of time before I had to go. All I had to do was find work that paid enough to keep my children and me. I got myself a job selling new homes, but the pay was low and wouldn't nearly have covered the rent on a flat.

A friend I'd made when I'd first moved to Sussex had a spare room and said if things got desperate the boys and I could live with her and her husband Todd until we found somewhere else. It was good to know we had a bolthole to escape to if Tom did lose his temper or hit me.

Although I thought Todd was great and I noticed that the two of them got on well, Josie confided in me that their marriage had been on shaky ground. I thought it a shame, especially as they seemed so right for each other. Josie had left Todd before, but returned for the sake of their two daughters. A few years later they did in fact divorce, but they managed to remain the best of friends. It's nice to know that people can split amicably, without dirty tricks and bitterness taking their toll.

Josie and I spent much of our time together, and the children and I were forever in her house, avoiding Tom. We kept up our morale by having a good moan about our husbands - Josie picking on Todd's annoying habits and me accusing Tom of being a bad-tempered control freak with a darts obsession.

'There's no bloody way I'm getting involved with another bloke,' was my mantra. Josie would nod and agree. She'd married young too and we wondered how our lives would have turned out if we'd remained single. We talked of what it might be like to travel, to go to college or to paint the town red every night.

Josie was as excited as I was when I got a reply from a music publisher about 'Passion'. He was well known in the industry and I couldn't believe he wanted to meet me to discuss my song. We got on very well from our first meeting in his London office, and he often took me to fancy restaurants and told me I was going to be a 'rich bitch' one day. 'Andrew', as I'll call him, didn't care about my age and colourful past; in fact, he said that many famous singers had had strange upbringings and had gone through abusive relationships, yet it hadn't harmed their careers in the slightest. It gave the newspapers something to gossip about.

'It's all about publicity, my dear,' he said, puffing on his cigarette and beckoning towards the waiter as we sat in another swanky restaurant.

Although I was happy that the publisher had taken an interest in my song, I wasn't entirely sure that it was just my music he was after. Andrew was much older than me, and I already knew he had a long-term girlfriend. I made sure he was aware I was married, not telling him that Tom and I had separate rooms.

One night he took me along to a gig to see a band he was thinking of taking on. He said it was all part of my learning process and that the experience would do me good. I was so excited, wondering if I was finally on my way to singing success. Not that Andrew had done much to help my career at this point, but if he wanted me to hang out with other musicians I thought it meant that he was actually taking me seriously.

I was dressed to kill that night, in a dress that left nothing to the imagination. Andrew's eyes were riveted to my non-descript cleavage and I was glad when the lights dimmed and the band came on to play their set. As we were listening to the final track, the promoter and DJ came over to chat to Andrew and me. The DJ was also well known, but I think it's best to just carry on calling him DJ.

DJ and I got talking and I don't know whether it was my being silly and star-struck; impressed that he was flirting with me, or whether his charm was winning me over, but I was quite taken with him. He wasn't the most attractive guy I'd ever met but we got on well and I ended up giving him my number, which didn't please Andrew at all. I told myself that my private life had nothing to do with Andrew, and, within a few weeks, DJ rang and invited me to the radio station where he worked.

The weather the next day was beautiful and my friend Belinda and I climbed into my open-top car, put on our sunglasses, turned up the radio and sped down the motorway towards the radio station.

Our hair flew in the breeze and we sang along to chart songs, feeling young and free again. My boys were with Mum, which had annoyed Tom because he didn't know where I was going or what I was up to and, yet again, I'd had to remind him that we weren't a couple any more and that we could both do as we wanted. Tom was quite at liberty to go on dates with other women, hang out in bars and clubs, or paint himself bright pink and dangle naked from a lamppost for all I cared.

When we arrived at the radio station, DJ invited us into the studio to see how everything worked. I was fascinated and felt very important, being allowed into the place that only the professional team at the station could enter. While we were there, DJ introduced us to his friend and co-presenter on his show, who seemed to take a shine to Belinda. Belinda made it more than clear that she wasn't interested and I told her off on the drive home for being so aloof. I didn't want her spoiling my chances with DJ or my budding pop career.

It didn't make any difference, because DJ and I carried on seeing each other and grew very close. He'd come down to the area where I was living and take me to dinner and we'd go on long drives, laughing and shrieking at his endless silly jokes or singing along to the radio. DJ had a lousy singing voice that made me laugh myself hoarse. It was a refreshing change to have some fun again: I couldn't recall the last time Tom and I had laughed together or had a carefree day out:

I didn't see my relationship with DJ as adultery because Tom and I weren't an item anymore. Yes, we were still married, but we'd been living separate lives for a while and it wouldn't be long before the boys and I would be off. I suspected that Tom would find someone else too. I just didn't envy the poor girl who ended up with him though.

I got on with looking after Lee and Shane and seeing DJ as often as I could. I'd tune into his radio show and listen out for his private little messages to me; 'I fly' meant 'I fucking love you' and then he'd play one of our favourite songs. I thought DJ was the best radio presenter I'd ever heard, but he was insecure and constantly fretted that his performance hadn't been up to scratch. I'd reassure him and he'd lap up my compliments, particularly when I said what a star he was. I hoped that some of his success - along with Andrew's backing - would rub off on me and that I'd be on the radio too.

Soon I introduced Shane and Lee to DJ and we drove to the seaside, where he was doing a road show. Josie came along as well.

That morning Tom had been his usual awkward self and demanded to know where I was going and with whom. His rants were growing worse by the day and he'd stopped playing as much sport, which did nothing to help the strained atmosphere in the house. Of course I lied and told him I'd promised the boys a day out at the seaside. Tom's eyes narrowed into slits and I could tell he was getting suspicious.

Tom had already met DJ leaving our home, but he'd assumed that I only knew him through my music and he didn't realise there was anything between us. Although, at that point, DJ and I hadn't taken things further and were actually platonic.

DJ was busy with his road show, so we didn't get to spend much of the day with us, but he made a fuss of the boys and played our favourite tracks. His co-presenter, who read the sporting news, was also there and this time he took a liking to my friend Josie and they both got into deep conversation, really hitting it off. They even went as far as arranging to keep in touch. Josie was full of excited chatter as we strolled around the fun fair, taking the kids on rides and feeding them candyfloss.

Shane was loud and boisterous that day, rushing about

and taking in every sight and sound. I was thrilled to see him so happy again - like the lively little boy he had used to be.

The boys were exhausted after their long day out and Lee was fast asleep in my arms as we walked back to my car. I placed him on the back seat with Shane, who was asking when we could come back to the seaside. I promised we'd return soon.

As soon as I got back to the house Shane made his way to bed and I settled Lee down. When I turned to go downstairs and get a drink from the fridge, Tom was standing, blocking my way. His mouth was pinched and his breathing heavy.

'Where the fuck have you been?' he shouted and flew towards me.

I reminded him that I'd told him I was taking the kids to the seaside. I took a step or two backwards, hoping to make an escape if Tom went to hit me. My mind was everywhere and that old feeling of terror came flooding back, making my heart pound and the blood rush to my face. I began to sweat and shake as Tom inched closer.

'You're a lying bitch!' he said, prodding me in the chest with his finger.

'Please, God,' I thought. 'Don't let him hurt me.'

But my prayers had come too late: Tom grabbed me by the hair and dragged me into his room, where he threw me onto the bed, punching me repeatedly in the face, until I couldn't even feel the blood that oozed from my nose and lips onto his duvet. He punched me until I could hardly feel my head at all and my vision was so blurred that the room seemed to melt into the distance.

'Tom…' I mumbled. 'Please…stop…'

'Die, you lying fucking whore!'

The punches continued to rain down on my face and body, then I felt his hands go around my throat and squeeze tight, shaking my head up and down so that it bounced against the bed. I had a flashback of the time that Luke had done the same and I began to feel the life draining from me. I didn't have the strength to struggle, so I just prayed that death would come quickly.

At that moment Shane came into the room, and I shudder every time I remember the look on his little face. Tom let go of me for a moment, I struggled to my feet and told Shane to go and lock himself in his room. As Shane turned to run, urine dripped down his legs and around his feet. Tom started to make his way towards him.

'No!' I shouted. 'Leave Shane alone! Run, sweetheart! Run! Run!'

Seeing Tom getting closer, Shane sprinted to his bedroom and I heard the door slam behind him. Tears flooded over my cheeks and I thanked God that my boy hadn't been hurt.

Tom came back and leaned over me. He raised his fist and was just about to punch me when I suddenly felt a calmness flood through me, and in the most soothing voice I could muster I repeated twenty times over that I was still in love with him and regretted the way I'd treated him; that I'd be a good wife again.

Tom studied my face, unsure of whether to believe me or not. He didn't say anything and hardly moved, until Lee woke up crying and Tom jumped up and went to the next room, where I heard him tell Lee to go back to sleep and said he'd see him in the morning. I wondered if he was going to read Lee a bedtime story, his voice was so normal. I couldn't believe he was acting as if everything was fine after he'd almost murdered me. It was surreal.

All I wanted to do was wash the sickening metallic taste of blood from my mouth and clean myself up, so I dragged myself to the bathroom, holding onto the walls as I made my way there to survey the mess that was once my face. It wasn't pretty and I turned away, unable to take in what I'd seen.

Soon, I felt someone standing behind me and turned around to find Tom with his fist pulled back and clenched, ready to punch me again. I fell to the floor as his fists pummelled my jaw, my cheekbones, my chest and my stomach.

'You disgusting fucking whore!' Tom screamed. 'You lying piece of shit!'

'Tom! Stop...please.'

He must have been hitting me for ages when I knew I had to do something to stop him or I was going to die. My face and body were numb, blood had run into my eyes, blocking my vision and breathing was difficult.

I could hear Shane crying in his room and I desperately wanted to go and comfort him. Somehow I found the strength to push Tom away from me and I yelled as loudly as I could that I loved him and that the violence must stop.

'I know I've been bad and I'm sorry,' I continued through swollen lips. 'I'm sorry. I love you so much, Tom, Please.'

This quietened him and he held on to his bruised fist for a moment, then stood up and made his way downstairs.

Filled with relief, I felt myself begin to drift off into blackness, but Shane's crying brought me back to my senses. I had to call a doctor too.

I don't know how I managed it, but I pulled my throbbing body down the stairs, picturing the receiver in my hand. Unfortunately the phone was in the living room, where Tom was sitting in his favourite chair, staring into space and rubbing his purple fist.

Blood from my nose trickled into my mouth as I pleaded with Tom to ring the doctor. Tom refused, telling me to clean myself up, but I insisted that my injuries were serious and that I had to get proper treatment. Almost falling into unconsciousness, I keeled over onto the sofa, coughing and clutching at my stomach, and Tom realised that I was in a very bad way and made the call.

Chapter Sixteen

The doctor arrived, took one look at me and eyed Tom in a way that made it clear that he knew what had happened.

Tom was sitting in his chair, clenching his fists on his thighs, daring the doctor or me to speak with his expression. The doctor picked up Tom's unspoken warning and busied himself examining me, announcing that he could do little for me at home and I urgently needed to go to hospital to be properly checked out. He went to call for an ambulance and, unbeknown to Tom or me, also rang the police.

The doctor stayed with me until the ambulance came, but Tom got angry when it turned up, refusing to let me see the boys before I left. I really wanted Shane to be with me, because I was scared Tom might harm him, but he gave me a firm 'no.' I hated the fact that Shane was shut in his bedroom, wondering if his mum was dead or alive. Knowing how much Tom favoured Lee, I was sure that he'd be safe with his dad, so I wasn't overly concerned for his safety at that point.

I asked the ambulance driver if he would mind stopping at Josie's place on the way to the hospital, as I really needed her support. It was very late when we arrived and it must have frightened the living daylights out of her and Todd. I could tell that she was trying to hold back her tears when she saw what a mess I was in.

'Bloody hell, Chez, I've seen you look prettier,' she said.

'Thanks,' I mumbled, too scared to laugh because my face hurt so much.

When I got to the hospital I was examined, and was thankful to find out that beneath the severe bruising on my face and around my neck I'd escaped with a dislocated jaw and needed five stitches above my left eye. After the doctors had finished I went to the loo and looked in the mirror. Josie was at my side.

'In a few days make-up might cover most of it,' she said, staring at my reflection in the smeared glass.

'Jo darlin', I don't care. At least I've still got my teeth, and I'm alive,' I answered.

When I got back to casualty I found two police officers waiting for me. They saw the mess I was in and urged me to come down to the station to make a statement. Armed with a cartload of painkillers, I was taken to the police station, but I refused to press charges, frightened I'd make the situation worse and risk Tom beating me again. When I look back I think how stupid I was and wished I'd taken him to court; he deserved to be punished for his actions. The problem was that any trace of strength or courage had left me and all I wanted to do was get my children as far away from Tom as possible.

I'd begged the police to go to the house and get Shane and he was brought to me at the police station. I felt so guilty when he looked at my bruised and stitched face. I was his mother - wasn't I supposed to protect him from the bad things in life? I'd badly failed him and Lee.

Shane hugged me and burst into tears, and I cried too, telling him how much I loved him and that I was okay.

'But look at the state of you, Mum,' he said.

We hugged and cried together for a long time, and then,

hand in hand, we made our way to Josie and Todd's place, where we'd arranged to stay for a while.

Josie and Todd were still having their own problems, but they buried their differences to care for us. DJ and his friend Rick came too, and they did their best to ensure that we were looked after and safe. I'll never forget how good those four people were to us. They couldn't have done more if they'd tried.

DJ and Rick stayed with me at Josie's house for a few days. They all waited on me hand and foot, and even bathed my cuts and bruises, to my embarrassment. I was a real sight and wasn't particularly happy about people seeing me resembling Lennox Lewis after a fight.

It wasn't long before Tom turned up at Josie's place, banging on the door and shouting to be let in to see me. Not wanting him to find men in the house, I pushed DJ and Rick out of the back door and told them to get away as fast as they could. Though I could hear Tom almost smashing the door in, I couldn't help laughing as I saw the two men desperately trying to clamber over the garden fence: Rick had his leg in plaster from a sporting accident and was on crutches, so getting over the fence was quite a feat. Josie and I hid until the police answered her phone call and turned up. However, because I hadn't pressed charges against Tom earlier, nothing was on record and the police couldn't take action against him for merely being an annoyance. He'd used threatening language, but technically he hadn't acted in a way to warrant being arrested.

Tom listened to the warning he got from the police and didn't return, but I was dreading speaking to him on the phone about Lee, and my fears were proved when Tom told me that I could take Lee to and from school if I wanted, yet I would never have custody of him.

'I'm the boy's father and he stays with me,' he said before slamming the phone down.

I didn't know what to do. I was frantic to get Lee back with me where he belonged and I was scared that Tom might lose his temper and take it out on our son. I spoke to Josie about employing a solicitor and applying for full custody, but Shane was so petrified of Tom that I couldn't even consider my ex continuing to be involved in our lives. All someone had to do was mention Tom's name and Shane would shake from head to foot. I tried to comfort him the best I could, reminding him that we were safe and that no one would hurt us again.

The thought of Lee living permanently with Tom was unbearable and although I was fairly sure he wouldn't hurt his own flesh and blood I couldn't be positive that the situation wasn't going to push his temper to its limits, putting Lee in danger.

'You know, Mum, Tom won't hurt Lee, at least not now. You wait till he's about seven or eight, and starts answering back, that's when he might,' Shane said.

I tried to stay as calm as possible and sat down to have a good think, praying for guidance. I had to keep my spirits up and with my auntie and friends behind me all the way I thought I was lucky I was to have such a network of support.

DJ had been so kind to me throughout the bad times, and Josie and I loved listening to his show, eager to hear his special messages and the songs he'd play for me. It cheered me up, knowing that he was thinking of me when he should have been concentrating on his job. Josie and I actually had a separate phone line installed, just so DJ could talk to me during commercial breaks.

Soon DJ suggested that Shane and I move in with him. I was relieved to have a refuge, but I was sad to leave Josie, especially as she was so unhappy in her marriage. We'd become very close and I was grateful that she'd stood by me, offering Shane and I a home. Still, I wasn't enthusiastic about being a burden, as I felt I'd been to Auntie and other members of my family.

DJ's flat was in a small town outside Oxford, a beautiful part of the countryside, where I felt I could gather some strength, so I accepted his offer. It didn't take long for us to settle in - we were surrounded by music and more music, which was great. Soon I began painting the flat and made it feel a little more like home, adding feminine touches here and there.

'What about Lee? When's Lee coming to be with us?' Shane constantly asked.

It was painful to hear my son fretting about his brother, and although I tried to reassure him as best I could, I was having a hard time ignoring my own doubts as to Tom's state of mind and his treatment of Lee. But however many phone calls I made to Tom to discuss what was going on, the more stubborn he became and the fewer visits he allowed. I had a hunch I'd have to face Tom in court if he didn't back down.

Shane had a room of his own, started at a new school in

the town where DJ lived and was always out playing with his new friends. It was fantastic to watch him running about and kicking his football in the street with them.

All we needed was some money to buy food and essentials, to pay our way. I wasn't expecting DJ to fund us on top of everything else, but Tom announced he'd increased our mortgage without telling me and refused to give me any cash, saying I could keep my car and that was it. Shane and I had no choice but to live off of my credit card. It seemed that my life was going around and around in circles.

While Shane was at school I spent most of my time with DJ at his radio station, or temping. Sometimes I got to help out with the shows and I hoped that my song 'Go on, Girl' might lead to a better and more affluent life for my kids and me. I worked hard promoting it, along with Andrew, who was now my manager. My relationship with him wasn't going too well though, because he wanted me to lie about my age to people in the business and deny that I had children. I didn't mind cutting five years off of my age – what woman would? Only there was no way I was going to pretend I wasn't a mother and go gallivanting on tour. Shane had had enough upset and I had no intention of deserting Lee either.

Andrew and I had stern words, him moaning that he'd put a lot of time and effort into my career and that I was ungrateful, not to mention unrealistic. I pointed out that I'd been honest with him all the way along, that I had two young boys and wasn't some hot, young thing in her early twenties with no responsibilities apart from choosing what boob tube to wear on stage. DJ wasn't impressed with my attitude either, and thought I was mad to put my family before my big break. He went on and on about how competitive the music industry was and how I should be more professional like him.

Although DJ had been caring at first, he changed when we started living together and I soon found out that he was completely obsessed with his job, the way he looked and what his fans thought of him. He continually asked me for reassurance as to how talented he was.

'Yeah, today's show was one of your best,' I'd nod. 'You've got such a great voice.'

He spent ages deciding which shirt to wear and would preen in front of the mirror, checking for creases and asking me if he looked fat. In reality, I was the one putting on weight. Every time we went out I'd watch him chatting up other women, no doubt trying the same lines he'd used on me when we first met. When I think about it now, I wonder if he had the odd fling or two during the period we were together: I found a couple of scribbled phone numbers in the bedroom and he'd often disappear, without telling me where he was going.

I never said anything to DJ about his flirtatious behaviour or asked what he was up to because by then I knew that I wasn't in love with him. I don't think I had the energy to love anyone at that point, so it wasn't DJ's fault. He had a few annoying habits – as we all do – but he was a nice man really.

It was more than obvious that DJ was losing interest and he didn't care about my problems with Tom. He just couldn't cope with all the emotional baggage I had bought with me. On several occasions he actually sulked because I didn't give him enough attention or hadn't tuned in to his show that day. It was as if I had three sons to think of, not two. I felt very alone, even though I spoke to Josie a lot and my dad and Auntie who were on the other end of the phone if I needed them.

The time drifted by, with me simply existing from day to day, taking Shane to school, listening to the radio, doing chores, or temping. On the days I was working, DJ was supposed to pick Shane up from school, but often forgot, leaving Shane to make his way home on his own. I was on automatic pilot, just doing what I felt should be done and then blotting out my worries with sleep, which was full of bad dreams. As the weeks passed my state of mind worsened until I couldn't make any sense of anything. I began to feel distant even from Shane and if that wasn't bad enough, I was losing my ability to cope with everyday activities as well. I'd forget what I'd just said and was forever forgetting to do simple tasks. My depression deepened and an unnerving event made me finally admit that I needed help. I was driving home in my car, when out of the blue I forgot where I was going, where I lived or who I was. I pulled the car to a stop and sat motionless for ages.

'Where are you?' I asked aloud countless times, banging the steering wheel with my fist. 'Come on, think!'

I decided that all I could do was to drive until my memory kicked in again. It was so frightening, making my way along a strange road with no destination and no sense of time or reality.

'Is it some kind of breakdown?' I thought, tears flooding down my cheeks and I stared out at the trees and houses that rushed past. Then as quickly as it had disappeared, my memory came back and I recognised a sign for a nearby town. I turned my car around and drove to DJ's house.

DJ wasn't home, so I rang him at work, needing to talk to someone close to me. He was in the middle of a show and couldn't come to the phone, so I took a deep breath and rang the doctor. He tried to calm me down and then said that I'd be okay until the next morning, when I should visit him during surgery hours.

I slept badly that night and was glad when daylight came and I could speak to my doctor. He said I was mentally exhausted and had to go to bed and sleep, for days if need be. He handed me a prescription for sleeping pills and I went to the chemist before returning home. There I looked at the sleeping pills and threw them angrily across the bed.

'Jesus, Cheryl, is this what you've come to, taking fucking sleeping pills.' I was so angry with myself. I never did take those tablets. Somehow I had to get through it all and face my demons without the aid of pills.

DJ didn't show much concern or go out of his way to talk to me and he still expected me to have sex with him when I woke up during my three days of almost continual sleep. I'd made sure that I was there for Shane, and I explained what was happening to me.

'It's okay, Mum, don't worry about me, I'll be alright,' he said. He'd had to grow up so quickly. He found DJ's old keyboard and kept himself amused by teaching himself how to play.

After that period of rest I woke to find I had a renewed strength and was ready to face up to the next stage of my life. It's amazing what a healing effect sleep has when your mind and body are completely exhausted. My head felt clearer and I sat down alone and went over all that had happened and thought about where I was going. At last I knew what I had to do.

Yet again, I'd relied on a man to make me feel wanted, useful and normal - whatever that was. Since the age of eighteen I'd bounced from one disastrous relationship to another, desperately trying to fill in the gaps. I'd looked to others to make my days complete, hoping for some kind of fairytale existence away from the harshness of life, and having done that my sense of reality was warped and I was attracting the wrong kind of people.

I was ashamed of my stupidity and told myself it was about time I bucked up my ideas and stood on my own two feet. I had to look inside *me* and not worry about pleasing others or what they thought of me, or gauge my self worth on how I was treated by people. I needed to recapture some of my old confidence and shed the insecurities that my past mistakes had heaped upon me. This meant I would have to go it alone for a while – with just Shane, and hopefully Lee too.

It was often difficult to remain strong because I was constantly hassled by Tom and I told DJ that I thought it best that we separated for a while. Although he was upset he didn't stand in my way and did all he could – along with his company and business manager – to help me secure a mortgage. I decided to move back near to where Josie lived.

Shane could return to his old school and hopefully pick up with his old friends. I knew the area and felt secure having people around me that I was familiar with. The flat wasn't far from where Tom was either, but I was ready to face my demons, and I didn't see why we should be driven away by my ex.

Shane was a stroppy fourteen-year-old by now and had ideas of his own: he loudly announced that he didn't want to move again - particularly not to be near Tom. However, with a bit of persuasion by promising to buy him a new keyboard he accepted the situation.

I was still broke and had to sell my car to raise the deposit for a flat, reminding myself that everything would turn out okay and that I mustn't waste energy stressing over finances. It was just as well I was a bit on the reckless side or I'd never have taken the risk. I did wonder how on earth I'd pay the mortgage when I didn't even have a job.

Using my powers of persuasion, I completed contracts within two weeks, and Shane and I were off again. We packed boxes with our belongings and hired a van for the rest, and after a long, tiring day we flopped onto the sofa, looking around at our new home in awe. Mum had been really good to me and helped us move in, and I was proud to see that she seemed impressed by my choice. It was such a lovely apartment and I was proud that I'd managed to do something right for once.

I couldn't believe the amount of wardrobe space I had and was excited to have my own room and a place to hang my clothes, without having to share with Tom and his cricket gear or DJ and his music collection.

DJ liked the flat too and offered to pay one hundred pounds a month towards the rent in return for the hours I'd spent helping him redecorate his place months before. I gratefully accepted, although I did feel as if I was using him and wasn't proud of myself for taking his money. It was time to get off my backside, find a job and be the independent woman I'd dreamed of being.

My relationship with DJ continued to limp along: on several occasions I tried to tell him that we weren't going anywhere, but he'd cry, persuading me to try again. I should have followed my instincts and cut ties with him altogether, yet DJ had been kind and I was a soft touch. I kicked myself for my lack of backbone afterwards.

It was wonderful to be living in my own place with Shane and he settled in straightaway, catching up with his old friends at school and driving me mad with his keyboard. Life got even better for us when Lee was allowed to spend weekends at the flat: Tom preferred to be throwing darts or making a spectacle of himself on the cricket pitch.

Soon my first mortgage payment was due and there were all the credit card payments on top of that. After an unsuccessful morning job-hunting, I decided to pop into the shop where I had worked some time ago to see an old friend. It was while I was there that I bumped into someone else I'd met years before, Serena.

Chapter Seventeen

Serena was very attractive, with her bright red hair, immaculate dress sense and perfectly manicured nails. She was about five years older than me, but where as I was all short skirts and long dangly earrings, she was like something out of the soap Dallas. She told me how she had once had an affair with an ageing executive from a leading airline company, who had set her up in a plush flat in the Barbican and kept her in absolute luxury. That's why she had such lovely jewels and clothes. Unfortunately, he returned to his wife and family to the country when he retired.

'You know, darling,' she drawled in her posh voice, 'he once asked me what I wanted for Christmas and I said a new pair of tits, my dear, would be most welcome. And here they are!' With that she proudly lifted her top and prodded them. 'See darling, aren't they wonderful?'

I thought Serena was hysterical and was glad to have found her again. She asked me if I'd been 'up to anything interesting', so I filled her in about the violent husbands and divorces and my attempt at being a pop star. She laughed hysterically, slapped the counter with her gold-ringed fingers and said she couldn't believe I'd got myself into such trouble. Eventually she did calm down and said she had an idea that could be of benefit to me.

Her new boss was on the look out for someone to market empty buildings, which was a bit of sideline for him, and she wondered if I might consider such a job. I didn't need to think twice and before she'd finished her sentence I asked her when I could start.

Serena and I swapped numbers and it wasn't long before she rang to say an interview was arranged for a few days later. I went along to meet her boss, we got on well and he told me I'd got the job. Later Serena phoned to tell me that although her employer did like me, he wasn't happy about my dangly earrings, which I'd only put on to liven up my black business suit. He wanted me too look more formal, so the earrings had to go – much to my disappointment.

The building I was going to sell was like a huge warehouse and was practically empty. All I had to do was to get a desk and a few bits of office equipment delivered, and dot plants around so the atmosphere wasn't as stark. Because the place was so spacious the acoustics were great and in between making calls to prospective clients I'd parade around, singing at the top of my lungs.

The job was only for six months, but after paying my first month's mortgage and my credit card bills I was extremely proud that I was independent. I stopped worrying and concentrated on enjoying my newfound freedom.

Shane was having a ball too. We spent many nights singing along to our favourite records, and he'd often go off for a game of football in the park with his mates. Mostly he stayed in his room practising the keyboard for hours, yet as great as everything was, we both felt that something or someone was missing from our lives and wished that Lee could be with us full-time, rather than just weekends.

DJ had been spending some time with me, but it was clear that we were going to go our separate ways, and he was busy with his shows and hectic social life.

It was during my first month in my new job that a young sales rep came to see me, trying to sell me office equipment I didn't want. After I'd refused his sales pitch he said something strange. He asked me if I'd go to a concert with his boss, reassuring me that he was a kind and generous man, but was a little low, having split up with his wife. Don't ask me what on earth I was thinking, as I was in no mood for dating men, but the rep came across as very genuine, so I agreed to go.

'I don't want any funny business.' I pointed my pen at him. 'Just friends, nothing else.'

The rep agreed and went on his way, and a week later an older man with striking blue eyes walked into my office, held out his hand for me to shake and introduced himself as Nigel. He had a lovely smile and as we shook hands my bangles clanked together, making Nigel laugh at the noise. He commented on my taste in jewellery, I brewed some coffee and we chatted for ages about all sorts of topics that had nothing to do with work.

Nigel was easy to chat to and also gave off an air of quiet strength. He wasn't a chatterbox like me, but what he did say was interesting and well thought out. I hoped he'd want to see me again.

A few hours later he said he had to go but asked if he could pop back to say hello another day. I nodded and off he went. I remember thinking that he wasn't that keen on me, that I obviously wasn't his type and put the meeting to the back of my mind; after all, the last thing I wanted to do was to get involved.

A week later Nigel did come back and we talked at length of our previous relationships and our children. Nigel had a girl of almost twelve, Jo and a boy of fourteen, Chris. He'd split up from their mother a few months before and was on fairly good terms with her, which meant he didn't have to haggle about visiting rights and the like.

Towards the end of our long conversation, Nigel appeared nervous, as if he was trying to say something, but couldn't pluck up the courage.

I thought that he was going to bring up the subject of the concert his rep had mentioned, and it was painful to watch Nigel tongue-tied and blushing, but sweet, none-the-less. To put him out of his misery I said that if he was trying to ask me out that I'd be pleased to accept. Nigel beamed and as he got into his car said he'd arrange an outing for the following week.

The night of our date arrived and I spent ages getting ready. I wore a red, velvet dress and even put on stockings and suspenders, though why I bothered I'd no idea because I had no intention of jumping into bed with Nigel, so he wouldn't get a glimpse of my underwear anyway. Feeling the pinch of the suspenders elastic I whipped them off and replaced them with tights. Forget sexy; being comfortable was more important.

Shane commented on the amount of effort I'd made getting ready and said that Nigel must be a special man for me to go to such lengths. I replied that it was the least I could do to go out looking presentable.

Nigel arrived right on time, looking dashing in a smart suit and new haircut. He said hello to Shane, pecked me on the cheek and led me to his car, a silver-blue Mercedes that gleamed so much under the street lighting that I asked him if he'd just had it washed. Nigel looked sheepish and tried to shrug my question off, but I was very touched that he'd gone to such trouble for me.

Nigel had booked a table at a Chinese place in Brighton and when we arrived we were met with a gorgeous restaurant that had a flight of steps leading to it. I felt so carefree in Nigel's presence that I grabbed his hand, dragging him as fast as I could towards the restaurant, almost toppling headfirst down the steps. Nigel's face was a picture and he puffed with exertion when we came to a stop. I was in fits, even if I had almost given him a heart attack.

He opened doors for me, held out my chair and poured my wine as we chatted over a candlelit meal. The evening flew by so quickly and after we left the restaurant he suggested we go for a stroll in Brighton's famous Lanes. I thought it all so romantic and was amazed when he asked if he could put his arm around my shoulders. A man had never treated me like that and, I must say, I liked it.

Soon it was time to go home and Nigel drove me back to the flat. It was a bit awkward because I wasn't sure whether I was meant to ask him in for a coffee, or if he was going to try and kiss me. But Nigel was still the perfect gentleman; he pecked me on the cheek, bade me goodnight and asked to see me the next day for lunch, before driving off.

One lunch led to another and Nigel and I became great friends. We didn't discuss anything more serious, as I wasn't about to run headlong into another relationship. I just enjoyed being with him, noticing more and more how he was so different from the other men I'd known. It was refreshing to be with someone who accepted me for who I was and would laugh at my silly sayings and habits, without putting me down or making me feel inferior.

DJ was still coming to my place at the weekends and though Nigel and I were still only platonic friends at that stage I felt awfully guilty, particularly as my liking for Nigel grew.

One night I returned from recording a demo at a studio in London and was about to put the tape on the stereo in the flat when it dawned on me just how much I was dying to be with Nigel. DJ was asleep in my bed, but I didn't want to wake him and play the track for him; I had to get Nigel to listen to it. It was his opinion I craved.

I rang Nigel and asked if I could come over to his place as soon as possible. I explained why and he agreed to see me, though I think he was very confused.

Borrowing DJ's car, I drove to Nigel's. He opened the door wearing a thick jumper and jeans and, looking incredibly handsome, a welcoming smile spread over his face. At that moment I realised I'd fallen in love with him and I hoped he felt the same way about me.

He was flattered that I'd asked him to hear my song before other people and said it was brilliant and what a good singing voice I had. We had a long conversation, during which we admitted our true feelings for each other, and I told Nigel I was going to speak honestly to DJ as soon as I got back to my flat.

DJ was awake when I returned, so I took the opportunity to come clean straightaway. It wasn't fair to carry on the way we had been and I hated the idea of hurting him. I admitted that I'd spent the evening with Nigel and that my emotions towards this other man weren't just platonic. DJ replied that he'd suspected something was amiss for a while and was hoping I might change my mind once I'd got Lee back and forgotten my past. The truth was that DJ and I were worlds apart; he wasn't a controlling or abusive man, but I couldn't love him. There wasn't enough of a connection.

With Nigel it was a different matter altogether. I felt as if I'd be safe and secure with him. Not that I wanted him to be a father figure; I just needed to be aware of the bad choices I'd made over the years and not travel down the same route again. I liked his quiet assuredness, which had a soothing effect upon me.

I apologised to DJ for not having more guts and telling him sooner, and after he shed a few tears, he got dressed and went on his way. It was very sad for both of us and I was filled with guilt, but we both knew we were going nowhere.

My six-month contract had flown by and soon I found myself worrying about finding work again. I needn't have though because good old Serena came to my rescue once more: the building she'd been marketing had been let to a foreign oil company and they were looking for someone to put the logistics in place. Many of their employees were to relocate from overseas and someone was required to find them housing and help them settle in. A few days later I went to the interview and was offered the job – along with a good salary – there and then.

Serena turned out to be a loyal friend and we're still in touch now. She married a rich man and spends her time reclining by her swimming pool in the grounds of her house in Texas.

Nigel and I celebrated my good news that night and he told me he was proud of me as we clinked champagne glasses. He also announced that his flatmate had met a woman and it was obvious that their relationship was serious, so it was time he found a home of his own. I wondered whether I should ask him to move in with me, but I'd been there too many times before and wasn't enthusiastic about taking such a risk. In the back of my mind I was a little tempted because I loved him very much, yet that warning voice in my head was holding me back.

So Nigel and I went hunting for a house for him, but each place we viewed wasn't exactly a palace and Nigel didn't fancy living in any of them, until eventually I guessed that he was stalling for time, hoping that I'd ask him to move in with me.

Just before Christmas, I changed my mind and said to Nigel, 'You can come and live here if you like, but I'll warn you now. I'm not getting married again.'

My divorce to Tom had come through months before and I didn't relish the idea of heading down the aisle, even with Nigel.

Nigel's face was a picture of happiness. He hugged me and gave me a big kiss before rushing to his flat to pick up his belongings. While he was gone I made some space in my wardrobe, my stomach churning with nerves, hoping that I wasn't being my usual hasty self. But I had a strong instinct that Nigel was different and that he'd never harm me or let me down.

It wasn't long before there was a ring at my doorbell and there stood Nigel with a bag of clothes and two pictures in one hand and a big orange wok in the other.

Shane pointed at Nigel's luggage, piping up 'Mum, I thought you wanted a rich man next time.'

'Shhh, big gob,' I wanted to say, but I smiled and led Nigel into the flat.

Shane was right though; Nigel did look poor and a little on the dishevelled side. His divorce had left him with next to nothing - even his pensions were useless. But as far as he was concerned he just wanted out and to make sure his kids were properly catered for.

We put his precious wok in the kitchen cupboard, found a place for the framed photos of his kids and hung his clothes next to mine. That evening the three of us shared a meal – cooked by Nigel – and settled down in front of the TV.

Chapter Eighteen

Nigel was supportive of my music and encouraged me to record my own CD. I decided to record three different kinds of songs on it, to show that I was versatile. What I didn't realise was that this was a bad idea when trying to break into the industry, as it gives the impression that the artist doesn't really know where they're going and hasn't discovered the right genre for them.

I worked with a respected keyboard player and thought one track in particular was smash-hit material, so Nigel and I approached the head of A&R at a big record company.

The man introduced himself as Simon Cowell and was seated behind a large desk in a rather plush office filled with plants and gadgets. I also noticed two large bins placed behind him and I asked what they were for, at which he picked up a tape from a pile and said, 'For this,' tossing it over his shoulder into one of the bins.

I felt sorry for the hopeful person who'd sent him their work and wanted to ask Simon why he hadn't even bothered to listen to their efforts. He looked bored and he introduced us to his sidekick, who was more approachable. The young man listened to my track, which he liked at once, encouraging Simon to give me a go. Simon sniffed and answered that he couldn't do anything with me even if the song was a seller because I was 'no spring chicken.'

I was dying to tell him where to stick my CD, but I managed to refrain from insults and Nigel and I muttered our goodbyes and left. I was livid and ranted about how shallow the music business was, until Nigel managed to persuade me that I was better than all that and that they were the ones who were missing out. Good old Nigel; he always found the right words when it came to lightening my mood.

After this letdown I invited my publisher Andrew to dinner so he could meet Nigel. They got on really well and Andrew was full of plans for my future, promising us both that soon I'd be a big star. Without being too immodest, I did have a good singing voice, but I guess Simon was right as far as the fickle music industry goes: I wasn't marketable.

Nigel was always my number one fan and he had a surprise for me that would take my mind off of my career disappointments and make me take stock of my personal life.

It was midnight on Christmas Eve and we were just about to go to bed when Nigel got down on one knee and asked me to be his wife. I wasn't expecting him to propose as I'd often said that I'd never marry again, but Nigel's face was so full of hope and I loved him so much that it took me about three seconds to change my mind and accept.

We both burst out laughing and kissed and hugged, before talking for hours about our wedding, our kids, how our families would react – especially mine, considering what a track record I had.

I decided I wasn't going to concentrate on the past. I was positive that Nigel was the right man for me and there was no way I was going to risk losing him.

I'd already met Nigel's children and although I got on fairly well with his son Chris, his daughter Jo was wary of me and the atmosphere between us was strained. She wasn't pleased that I'd 'stolen' her father and was clinging to the hope that her parents would get back together.

When Jo heard of our wedding plans she made it clear that she didn't approve and stormed out of the room. I was keen to mend our relationship and thought that if I asked her to be bridesmaid she might mellow a little. She did agree when I suggested the idea, but she wasn't as enthusiastic as I'd hoped and she still threw the odd dirty look my way when she thought I couldn't see her. I reminded myself to be patient with her and that one day she'd accept me. After all, she felt she had to be loyal to her mum, which was how it should be.

My patience with Nigel's ex wife was wearing a little thin though. He'd made sure the kids were looked after financially so it was very upsetting when derogatory comments came back to us via the kids. I felt terribly sorry for Nigel and wanted to go around and have a word with his ex, but he was never one for confrontation, nor would he discuss the situation in front of his children. Not once did he say a bad word about their mother and I really admired him for his loyalty, although I could have quite cheerfully throttled her at one point.

Eventually, as time passed, the situation calmed down and Nigel's ex wife agreed that when the children grew up and left home she'd sell their house and give half of the proceeds to Nigel. I wasn't entirely sure I believed her - after all, the law stated that she didn't have to put her home on the market or split the profits from the sale. I put the idea to the back of my mind and was just pleased that we were all being more amicable towards one another. I crossed my fingers that Jo and I would follow suit and at least try to be friends.

I wasn't remotely worried about the strength of Nigel's and my relationship, yet marriage was a huge step and one that frightened me. I didn't speak to Nigel about my fears and tried to ignore them, but it wasn't long before we both realised just how dramatically my past had affected me.

One evening we decided to go to the cinema, and because there wasn't much else being shown we bought tickets for 'Sleeping with the Enemy,' which starred Julia Roberts as an abused wife. The film began and I cringed as I watched the leading actor doing exactly as Luke had, ordering Roberts' character to fold the towels in a certain way and checking the kitchen cupboards to see if the tins were straight. When the woman was getting a beating, I put my hands to my face and squinted through my fingers, hoping it would soon end.

When the lights went up and we walked outside to the car I was silent and Nigel turned to me and asked if I was okay because I looked shaken.

'Of course I'm bloody shaken. I've just watched my own life being played out in front of my face,' I answered.

Nothing more was said and as we drove home my thoughts were on Luke and Tom, and the lucky escape I'd had. I'd been reminded that I could well be dead and I wondered if it was wise to risk getting married again. Luke and Tom had seemed kind at first and they'd changed overnight. What if Nigel did the same?

I glanced at Nigel's profile and told myself that he was a gentle, considerate man who loved my kids and me, but there was a tiny, niggling doubt somewhere at the back of my mind.

When we got home I was still quiet and my thoughts were muddled, so I sat on the edge of the bed to remove my shoes, reassuring myself that I'd feel better after a good night's sleep. It was just as we were about to turn the light off that Nigel tried to improve the strained atmosphere by making a joke.

'Have you straightened the towels?' he asked.

The question was like a hard slap in the face and I went mad, yelling and swearing at Nigel. I was out of control, pacing the room and waving my arms in the air. Poor Nigel couldn't get a word in edgeways and was at a complete loss as to what to do. When he tried to touch me I pushed his hand away and rewarded his attempts at soothing me with insults.

Soon I'd exhausted myself with shouting and I flopped onto the bed, where I cried until there were no more tears left to shed. Nigel did his best to comfort me and said how sorry he was for making such a stupid remark, but I couldn't answer him and wasn't able to control my emotions.

When I finally calmed down I felt really silly for being such a drama queen.

'Sorry, Cheryl,' Nigel whispered and put his arm around me. 'I didn't mean to hurt you.'

'I know, love,' I sniffed and wiped my nose on a sodden tissue.

Nigel tucked me into bed and gave me a cuddle, and

when we woke up the next morning I cringed at the memory of the night before. I decided that I'd cook Nigel a nice meal after work or buy him a little token of my affection and when I went to get up I couldn't move my legs. There was no sensation in them at all and I cried out to Nigel that I thought I'd had a stroke.

Nigel was panic stricken and sprinted to the phone to call the doctor while I just lay there like a lump, unable to even sit up properly.

The doctor turned up pretty quickly and examined me, announcing that I had hysterical paralysis brought on by all the pent-up stress I'd stored throughout the years. The film had acted as a catalyst, unearthing my fears; and the doctor also told me that because I'd met a man I felt I could trust, my body was now releasing those damaging emotions. He reassured me that my condition wasn't permanent and that I had to rest until the feeling in my legs returned and I was able to walk again.

For a week I was paralysed and Nigel, bless him, had to carry me everywhere, lugging me to the toilet and back again. No wonder he suffered with a bad back. Nigel had proven his love for me, as well as nursing me, he'd spent hours listening to my song lyrics, playing with Shane and ensuring that we were cared for. My misgivings finally began to dissolve. I'd really put him to the test, often asking him when he was going to turn into a bastard, like all men. I'd acted as if I didn't care on many occasions and complained when I thought he was putting his job or others before me, even though he'd done no such thing.

Yet not once did he lose his cool or tell me off; he'd smile and say that he loved me and always would. He understood me, and I think he was waiting for the day that I'd fully trust him and not compare him to the rotten men from my past.

It was during these difficult times that some strange occurrences made me wonder if Ben was trying to pass me a positive message and calm my fears.

I loved 'I Have a Dream' by ABBA and I'd play it constantly, singing along, because I was to perform the track at my wedding. One morning, as I got ready for work, the CD kept stopping. Fed up with trying to get it to play again, I pulled the plug out of the socket, only to be shocked rigid when the song started again. I ran from the flat and sped off in my car, I was so scared.

Soon Shane began having weird experiences too: he'd be using his computer when the mouse would move about on its own or his keyboard would suddenly strike up a song, the keys being pressed by an invisible musician.

Nigel wasn't left out either and I thought he was about to have a heart attack one night when the door handle on our bedroom door started turning of its own accord. I checked to see if there was anyone trying to get in, but I was absolutely sure that it was Ben and knew he was happy for us all.

After a lot of hard work on Nigel's part, I was finally able to put my faith in him and we went ahead and booked the wedding. It was to be held in our local church on the sixth of July 1991.

Knowing that it was my wish to have a romantic ceremony, Nigel said that money was no object and that he wanted me to choose whatever dress I wanted, along with all the trimmings. I was like an over-excited young girl as I picked out my beautiful gown, made from ivory lace and dotted with pearls and diamante studs. It's a terrible cliché, but I felt as though I was Cinderella and couldn't wait for the day to arrive so I could float down the aisle with Nigel by my side, handsome in his posh suit and top hat. Even Lee and Shane were to have smart new outfits and shiny shoes.

I was frantically busy sending invitations to family and friends, designing my own flower arrangements and booking the reception, but I loved every minute of it. Nigel was swept along by the excitement too, him having got married in a registry office the first time around.

Another thrilling aspect of this period was that a DJ on a local radio station mentioned my song 'Go On, Girl'. This seemed really funny to me - after all, I wasn't exactly pop star material. He also mentioned my upcoming marriage. How he had found out I wasn't entirely sure though.

Our wedding day dawned, and as Nigel and I came to a halt outside the church in a horse-drawn carriage I felt like a celebrity. It turned out that people in our town had read an article about my song in the paper, which had run a headline along the lines of 'Local Artiste Gets Married'. There was a small crowd cheering us on and I was touched that strangers had made such an effort.

I looked at Nigel and laughed when I saw that the colour had actually drained from his face. Nigel was never one for being the centre of attention and neither was the vicar, who voiced his surprise at the turn out.

I was pleased that Auntie and some of my family were

attending the ceremony, but I was disappointed that Dad couldn't make it from Australia because the airfare was too expensive. He did call and wish me luck though, saying that he hoped I'd be happy with Nigel.

I stepped off the carriage and as Shane was to give me away he was at my side to help me down onto the pavement, and then with 'Bat out of Hell' by Meatloaf blaring out, we walked into the church.

Auntie Joyce smiled at me and I hoped she felt proud, knowing Nigel well enough to see that I wasn't repeating past mistakes. I so desperately wanted everyone to like Nigel and see that I'd grown up. I was a sensible person now.

I walked down the aisle, accompanied by my son and Nigel grinned widely at me, taking in my beautiful dress. The vicar asked us to kneel, which was such a relief.

'My bloody feet are killing me,' I whispered to Nigel.

I'd spoken to Nigel about our vows, telling him that I couldn't say 'Until death do us part.' I'd said it to my other husbands and I felt as if I'd been a hypocrite. Instead, we decided that I should write our vows and I spent hours trying to come up with the right words.

On our wedding day Nigel and I said the following:

'I promise to respect you as an individual, to respect your needs and to be there for you. To not just hear but to *listen* to what you have to say, to stand by you, support and love you, even during those times when you need to be alone. I promise to encourage you in your hopes and dreams and, above all, to be your best friend and lover. This is my pledge to you, because of my love.'

Nigel's eyes gleamed as he repeated his vows and I choked back a sob, worrying that if I started crying I'd have mascara running down my face.

When the ceremony was over friends and family came to kiss us, they showered us with confetti, photos were taken and Nigel and I were whisked off in the carriage to our reception in a nearby hotel.

The reception wasn't exactly traditional, and one of the guests was a magician from 'The Sooty Show' who I'd booked to entertain the kids. While he was doing his act, Nigel and I posed for the photographer and were also glad that one of our friends had taken many snaps, giving us a less formal reminder of our day.

Dad couldn't be there, so Nigel had secretly written to him, asking him to put a message on tape. I was doling out gifts to the kids and other guests, and was about to go back to my seat, when I heard my dad's voice.

'Well, Cheryl, by now you're married. Nigel wrote to me and as Noreen and I couldn't be with you on this special day we thought this song was appropriate. Enjoy yourself. Love Dad and Noreen.'

'Celebrate my Love for You' followed and by the end of the track there wasn't a dry eye in the place, and with tears streaming down my face I kissed and thanked Nigel. But he hadn't finished there. The next voice to blare out of the hotel's stereo speakers was Dan's, the social worker who'd handled Shane's case. He was living in North America at the time and had recorded his message in the style of a DJ on the radio station WKLM. Dan wished us luck and got everyone to stand and toast the bride and groom. I looked around at our guests I saw that even the most macho of men were dabbing their eyes with tissues.

'I can't believe you went to all this trouble for me,' I sniffed to Nigel.

'I wanted this day to be really special for you, babe,' he sniffed back.

Later, I stood up and sang 'I Have a Dream' with my musician friends and the choir I'd booked, with Shane accompanying us on the keyboards. I was so proud of my talented son.

Some South African men who were staying at the hotel asked if they could join the party and I told them they were welcome. What I hadn't realised was that they were musicians too and they brought their guitars along, so all the guests spent the rest of the night singing along to Irish music and the blues.

It was well into the early hours of the morning when Nigel and I said our goodbyes and thanked everyone for a fabulous evening, before we went up to our room. I was so tired I flopped onto the bed, too exhausted to remove my wedding dress. Nigel and I were asleep almost as soon as our heads hit our pillows.

The next morning Nigel and I flew off to Portugal for our honeymoon and I think I must have smiled the whole way there. I remembered the times I'd got married before and I knew that it was different now. I felt like a proper newlywed.

I thought Portugal was stunning, with its' beautifully decorated villas, palm trees and colourful flowers that seemed to cover every wall in the town. The restaurants were so quaint, and that evening we dined on a moonlit balcony with the sounds of the sea serenading us. It was one of the most romantic times of my entire life, just as a honeymoon should be.

After our meal we realised it was getting late, so we sauntered back to our villa, where my new husband and I made up for our lack of passion on our wedding night.

Nigel decided he wanted a cup of tea and trotted to the kitchen, stark naked. A minute later he returned to the bedroom, pointing behind him and unable to speak. He was deathly pale.

'Kitchen…something in the kitchen,' he stuttered.

I did my best to calm him and eventually he managed to explain that he'd felt a presence that had made the hair on the back of his neck stand up. He asked me to go to check the kitchen with him, to see if I sensed the presence.

Hand in hand we tiptoed back to where he'd been and, sure enough, there was one particular spot that was ice-cold and I was absolutely positive that Ben had returned to send us a message; that he'd come to say goodbye.

I reassured Nigel that whatever it was wouldn't hurt us, without telling him who the invisible being was. Nigel wasn't used to having such experiences and I was afraid of scaring him.

With shaking hands, Nigel finished making the tea and we went back to bed, where we both relaxed enough to drift off to sleep.

It must have been a couple of hours later that I was woken by the sound of heavy footsteps on the marble floor of the villa. Gradually they got louder, until they came to a halt outside the bedroom door. I lay still, not daring to move, and glanced at Nigel, who was fast asleep, then turned my head towards the door again, waiting for it to open. Suddenly Nigel sat bolt upright and shouted, 'He's in my face! He's in my face!'

'Who is?' I asked, placing a hand on his shoulder.

Nigel said the man had blond hair and blue eyes and he went into great detail about the rest of his appearance. He had described Ben. The most disturbing aspect of the whole experience was that Nigel had never seen a single photo of Ben.

Nigel was very shaken and told me he'd also heard the footsteps. I felt I should tell him who our visitor was and why he'd come, and Nigel's eyes were as big as dinner plates as my story unfolded. Although we were unsettled by what had happened, it was a relief to know that Ben meant us no harm. He wanted us to be happy. That was the very last time I heard from Ben.

Chapter Nineteen

Shane had started music college, Lee seemed to be settled with his dad and I was thoroughly enjoying my job with the oil company. Married life was bliss and our lives plodded along very nicely, without one hint of a catastrophe.

That is, until I picked up the phone to hear my mother crying hysterically. Mum said that Sheena's daughter's boyfriend had made an indecent move on her and that she'd fled the house, calling him 'a filthy fucking bastard.'

The incident had frightened Mum greatly, so Nigel and I went around to her house to try and calm her down. When we got there, it was plain to see she was still in the state of shock. The young man hadn't touched her, but he'd been very descriptive and crude. Mum wasn't used to this kind of behaviour and was out of practice when it came to dealing with men's advances, which added to her distress. I made her a cup of tea and Nigel and I stayed with her until she felt better.

I thought that would be an end to the matter, since Mum hadn't been molested, but the next thing I knew Lucy had infuriated Mum by saying that she must have acted in a way to encourage the boy. I was very angry and couldn't understand why Lucy would accuse Mum of something like that. Mum was no angel, but she wasn't the type to try it on with her granddaughter's boyfriend.

I rang Lucy and asked why she'd made such a suggestion and, as arguments always do within families, it all became heated, the past was brought up and we both said things we shouldn't have.

Later that evening I was still seething and remembering the times Lucy had spread rumours about me and sent me those terrible letters filled with hate. I was sick of her judging others while she thought herself so perfect. Hadn't she had a child by her husband's friend? Poor Robert had no idea that Rebecca wasn't his and Lucy had no idea that I'd overheard Mum and Dad talking about the whole affair when I was a kid.

I was so angry that I was about to dial Lucy's number, intending to tell her that I knew all about her sordid secret. Nigel tried to make me see sense, but I wouldn't take any notice. Just as I was about to call Lucy, her eldest child Leanne rang and the conversation ended with me saying that her mother should look at her own life and stop judging other people. I put my boot in even further by dropping a hint that there was an issue concerning Rebecca that she didn't know about.

But Leanne surprised me. 'What? You mean that Rebecca's not my dad's?'

'Yes,' I mumbled and Leanne slammed the receiver down.

She must have been straight on the phone to her mum because I soon received a call from Lucy.

'You fucking cow! Why the fuck did you open your great big mouth? As far as I'm concerned you and Mum are dead. Do you hear me? Dead!' Then she hung up. I must state in fairness to Lucy that she has no recollection of the phone call, so we have since agreed to disagree regarding this point.

FOR CRYING OUT LOUD

Lucy hadn't let me explain my side of the argument – not that I would have come out of it in a good light, but I wanted to tell her that I'd known about Rebecca since I was twelve and had kept her secret for the sake of her and her family.

Mum was devastated that Lucy didn't want to know her; she'd had nothing to do with any of the phone calls or the accusations flying back and forth. She hadn't been the one who'd told me about Rebecca as Lucy assumed. Mum was blameless and I felt sorry for her.

I was kicking myself for having such a big mouth and I knew that, because of me, Lucy's life had been turned upside down. Not only would she have to come clean with her husband but she was also going to have to face Rebecca. My sister might have played some awful tricks on me in the past, but we'd managed to forget any wrongdoings and make up. I'd always tried to tell myself to forgive and not to hold grudges against others, yet it seemed that deep down I still held a lot of resentment towards Lucy.

Now it was my turn to be forgiven, so I hoped, and I wrote to Rebecca and Lucy, to give them my side of the story and offer my heartfelt apologies.

However hard I tried to sort out the whole sorry mess, the more I was ignored and it was to be years before we all spoke again.

My musical ambitions were still as strong as ever and I'd found myself a writing partner who'd once been in a well-known band. Together we came up with two tracks called 'Free the Spirit' and 'Voice in the Wind', about Shane leaving home and going off to college. I was proud of

Shane's achievement, but it had been such a wrench when he left home and I missed him a lot.

I reckoned that 'Free the Spirit' was good enough to be a number one dance hit and I was excited to be the lead singer on it. I had such faith in the track that I went to try and sell it to record companies.

One showed interest in the song, and Nigel and I went to London for a meeting, but when we got there a coincidence ruined my chances of pop stardom. Nigel and I entered the record company's offices and I at once recognised the song they were playing: one that had been written by my partner and the band he'd been in previously. For some reason a couple of the staff there began to look at me strangely and I blushed, thinking, 'Oh no, they can see I'm no spring chicken.'

Soon we were taken to the A&R man's office and he asked me if I was the singer on the track that was being played and I said I wasn't. He frowned and sat down to listen to my CD of 'Free the Spirit', which he loved. Something was still wrong, because he mentioned the other song again and from his expression I could tell that he was confused. I didn't stick around to ask questions and after the man had promised he'd be in touch. Nigel and I left, discussing how weird the day had been.

When we got home the phone rang and I picked up the receiver to hear my writing partner's angry voice. It turned out that his friends had lied to the record company, saying that their lead singer had written and was singing both the song I'd heard when entering the company and 'Free the Spirit', so they couldn't fathom why I'd said that I was the vocalist on 'Spirit'. It made my partner's friends appear unprofessional and the record company lost faith in them. We must have looked like a bunch of amateurs.

My writing partner shouted that I'd ruined his friends' chance of a record deal and that it was my fault.

'How on earth was I supposed to know you lot were piling on the bullshit with a trowel? I'm not psychic,' I pointed out.

I went on to tell him that if I'd known what they were up to I'd have gone along with the plan and said I wasn't the singer, but their dishonesty really upset and disappointed me. I'd trusted my writing partner and couldn't believe that our relationship had come to an end because of a misunderstanding that I'd had nothing to do with. I was left with the hope that 'Passion' might get me somewhere in the future.

Along with my music career, my job with the oil company soon folded. Nigel lost his job too, so we found ourselves accumulating large debts. Fed up with working for others, we decided to start our own office partitioning and refurbishment company, borrowing from family and scrimping and scraping for the money to get us started after the bank refused to help. It was a ridiculous set-up, with Nigel in the lounge and me working from the bedroom, trying to fathom out how to use a computer and making hundreds of phone calls to prospective clients.

It was a big step to take, and Nigel and I were worried that the business might not thrive, but we were willing to put in all the time and effort required to make a success of our venture. Not only was I concerned about our finances and how we'd fare in the corporate world, I was also extremely worried about Lee, who was eight by now. He was quiet and withdrawn, and when I asked him why he wasn't saying much, he'd shrug and reply that there was nothing wrong, he was just tired.

I decided that I keep a closer eye on him and persuaded Tom to let me take Lee swimming or to the park most nights, using excuses if I had to.

It was towards Christmas of 1993 that Tom's resentment of me, which was probably due to the fact that he knew I was suspicious of his treatment of Lee, came to a head and he rang and shouted abuse down the phone.

'You fucking whore!' He said in a voice slurred by drink. 'I hate you, you fucking whore!'

Nigel was sitting next to me on the sofa and he snatched the receiver out of my hand and told Tom that no one spoke to his wife in such a manner. Tom replied that Nigel didn't know what I was like and that I'd been a useless wife and mother. Nigel said he wasn't interested in the past or anything Tom had to say and that he was going to go around and have it out with him.

'No, Nigel!' I said. 'Tom's a madman.' There was no way I wanted him getting involved in the situation and being punched.

Nigel was adamant that we had to go and face Tom, so we drove to his house, dreading the reception we were going to get. And just as we thought, Tom was drunk and furious when he opened his front door. He shouted terrible insults and called me every name you could imagine.

'I should have finished the job off and fucking killed you

when I could, you useless whore!' Spittle flew into the air and Tom pointed his finger in my face.

Nigel and I kept our cool, knowing there was no point in trying to reason with someone like Tom, but my ex was ready for a fight and clenched his fist, intending to land a punch on Nigel's nose.

Nigel calmly took a step back, put a finger on his nose and said to me, 'I quite like this nose, don't you?'

I was trying not to laugh, especially when I saw Tom's reaction. He had no idea what to think or do and stood there looking lost, his fist hanging in the air.

Nigel then said that he knew all of Tom's cricket cronies and that if he didn't leave us alone he'd tell them he was a wife-and-child beater. At that time we weren't positive that Tom was hitting Lee, but we were determined to find out. He'd been a tyrant towards Shane and I wasn't prepared to let another son go through all that.

Nigel's threat did the trick and after denying that the incident ever took place, Tom kept his distance. He'd met his match in Nigel.

Our business was struggling to get off the ground and we were working morning, noon and night, so it was such a lovely surprise when I won a competition to a health spa in the Bahamas.

The spending money wasn't included and, again, Auntie and Uncle came to my rescue, saying that we deserved a break in the sun. Nigel and I told them that we'd pay them back as soon as we were on our feet.

Not only was our holiday a relaxing break from all the

stress we'd been through, it was also to bring me a surprise I've never forgotten. I got chatting to the owner of the local radio station and recording studio and mentioned 'Passion'. He asked me for a copy of the CD, which I took practically everywhere with me. He played it and did a live interview with me, and the track was a big hit with everyone on the island. I had lots of requests to buy it, but I didn't have any copies with me, or any way of reproducing it.

Our smiles weren't to last long, because when we got home we found out that the Child Support Agency had contacted Nigel's ex wife, as she was claiming social security. They accused Nigel of not paying enough maintenance for Jo and Chris and now wanted us to also support his ex. This infuriated us because Nigel always put his children first and made sure they were cared for financially: even paying for clothes, school trips and extra essentials and treats.

Next the CSA announced that I too should contribute towards Chris and Jo's keep, which was outrageous. I had stern words with Nigel's ex, who was just trying her luck, but she should have thought twice because it turned out that she was claiming benefit she wasn't entitled to. When it was clear there was proof of this fact, she got cold feet and told the CSA that she was happy with the original payment plan she had with Nigel.

Incensed by the experience and by the way the CSA operated, Nigel and I set up a support group for fathers who were being fleeced by greedy ex-wives and we received hundreds of letters and phone calls from men who'd lost their children and their home and were subsequently told they had to lose most of their wages too. Some of these poor men could hardly afford to pay rent or buy food, and some had to return to their parents or family with nothing, not even their self-esteem. Many had to haggle for visiting rights to add to their humiliation. The number of suicides I heard about was frightening, and Nigel and I did our best to offer what advice, comfort and support we could.

Unfortunately, there were so many men affected by the CSA's actions that we didn't have enough time or resources to help as many as we'd have liked. We thanked our blessings that we'd managed to come out of our own experience with a positive result.

One night, Nigel and I were watching TV or chatting, I don't exactly recall, when I had a phone call that sent me into panic mode. It was Tom's girlfriend.

'Cheryl,' she said, 'I had to ring and ask. Did Tom ever hit you?'

I didn't know the woman and the last thing I wanted to do was get involved, so I tried to be as cagey as I could. I felt sorry for her if he was beating her, but I simply couldn't face anything to do with my ex. That is, until she said, 'He gets angry with Lee a lot too.'

Nigel and I discussed calling the police, snatching Lee from school or just refusing to let Lee return home after his next visit with us, but we needn't have fretted because an hour or so later Tom's girlfriend was on our doorstep with Lee beside her. She handed Lee to me and then was gone.

I took Lee into the house, relieved to have him with me and away from his dad, and I bent down to give him a big hug, when he flinched.

'What's wrong, Lee?'

'My back's sore, Mum.' His face was very white and downcast.

I gently lifted his top and was horrified to find a big bruise in the shape of a footprint.

Holding back my tears, I asked Lee how he got such a bad bruise and he replied, 'Daddy kicked me in the back because I wasn't moving quickly enough when we were out walking.'

With more coaxing from me Lee went on to tell me about Tom bullying him for not doing his homework quickly enough and the times he'd been called 'stupid' and then slapped around. I could see that he was so scared of his father that he'd turned into a very unhappy little boy – like Shane had before him. How I wished I'd followed my gut reaction and done something sooner. What kind of mother was I? My two children had suffered at the hands of this man and what had I done? The awful feelings of guilt and self-recrimination returned and I knew I had to take action. I wasn't going to let anyone harm my boys again.

'You're going to live with us now, sweetheart,' I said as I looked into Lee's sad eyes. 'You're safe.'

Nigel and I secured an emergency security order and prepared ourselves for a custody fight with Tom.

Chapter Twenty

Once again I was locked in the middle of a never-ending circle of social workers, and Lee was placed on the at-risk register. And once again I had to answer endless questions about my child and the treatment he'd received at the hands of an emotionally abusive, violent man.

Shane was questioned about his experiences with Tom, after which the social workers had the audacity to express pity for my ex husband, stating he had a problem controlling his anger and could be helped with counselling. This really added insult to injury.

Court proceedings began. Nigel and I were working all the hours we could and because some earnings were coming in we knew it wasn't right that we should apply for Legal Aid. Tom, being freelance and devious with it, lied about his wage and basically pleaded poverty, so he was granted Legal Aid. This pleased him greatly and he was quite aware that Nigel and I could very easily lose our home and our business if the case dragged on.

Lee spoke to his dad and said that he wanted to live with me and that he didn't want his parents to go to court and fight over him, but Tom took no notice and wouldn't even let us collect Lee's clothes and belongings. All Lee had were the trousers and top that he was brought to us in.

At the first court hearing the judge ordered Tom to let Nigel and I go around to his place and pick up Lee's things, but Tom refused to abide by the judge's decision. We gave up in the end and went out and bought Lee a new wardrobe of clothes and a few toys.

It was during this outing that it hit home just how badly his father had affected Lee: he was eating an ice cream when he accidentally dropped it onto the pavement, and he looked up at Nigel with fear on his face. He thought that Nigel was going to tell him off for being clumsy or even hit him. I gave him a big cuddle and told him that it wasn't his fault he'd dropped his ice cream and that no one was angry with him. Lee was quiet and I could see that he wasn't sure whether to believe me or not.

Soon 1994 was upon us and with two adults and a child in my small flat it was very cramped, so we rented my place out and found a bigger and older property. We loved it there, and Lee began to open up a little and would play with his toys while Nigel and I sipped cheap wine and enjoyed long chats in the garden.

We were trying our best to keep our business together and still had a fight on our hands regarding Tom, as well as relentless questions and interference from social workers and the courts. But I had a feeling that Lee was home for good. I had to keep hold of that hope; it spurred me on.

While the custody struggle carried on I went to my doctor for a routine smear test and abnormal cells were found. I needed to go to hospital for more tests. I passed the letter to Nigel, who read it and then looked at me.

'Don't worry. You're going to fine, babe,' he said, giving me a hug.

I tried to put on a brave face for the sake of my family, but inside I was petrified and I wondered what else could go wrong.

'Why is my body now letting me down?' I thought.

Nigel and I went to the hospital and the results weren't what I was hoping for. I was in the early stages of cervical cancer.

I simply had no energy left inside me to cry and I tried to block the news from my mind. I think if I'd faced the truth and dwelt upon what the outcome could be, I'd have gone under and I knew I mustn't do that. I had a family to consider. I wasn't going to die.

So Nigel and I busied ourselves as much as we could with our growing business and I acted cheerful in front of Lee. The last thing he could cope with was the thought of losing his mum.

It wasn't until I went for the laser treatment that the truth of what was happening really struck Nigel and me. I lay on my back, staring up at the ceiling with my legs wide open and the doctor wielding his surgical equipment, and I felt a burning sensation deep inside me, searing through my body. I looked at Nigel's face and the fright I saw was incredible. The stench of burnt flesh soon filled the whole room, making me feel nauseous. Nigel avoided talking about what was happening and we tried to keep ourselves light-hearted with small talk, but it didn't work very well. We clutched hands tightly and looked into each other's eyes.

'I love you,' Cheryl,' Nigel said in a wobbly voice.

'I love you,' I whimpered.

Nigel drove me home, sore and tired, and I went straight to bed, as I'd been told by the doctor to rest. Nigel brought me my meals and fussed around me, making sure I was comfortable.

'I'm not bloody dying, you dopey sod,' I laughed. I just prayed that my words were true. I crossed my fingers and spoke to God, as I always did and I think it helped me to keep my strength and sanity.

I was still sprawled in my bed when Shane rang to announce that now his music course had ended he needed to come home for a while. I replied that was fine and that I couldn't wait to see him, and then he added that he wasn't going to be on his own; he was bringing his girlfriend, who needed a place to stay. Nigel and I agreed and Shane and his girlfriend moved in. It was a little cramped with the five of us, but I was glad to have my boys back together again and everyone generally helped out with the chores. I did often wonder if Nigel ever regretted taking such a troublesome bunch on. If he did, he never admitted it and he never complained.

A few weeks later we were driving to our office, when a blue chip company van crashed into the back of us with great force, sending us careering across the other side of the road.

I didn't really feel much, but soon I started to notice some discomfort in my neck, and after we'd swapped details with the driver of the other vehicle, Nigel took me to hospital, where x-rays showed that I had severe whiplash.

'Sweetheart,' I said, rubbing my neck as I sprawled on yet another hospital bed. 'I'm like a walking accident waiting to happen.'

Nigel drove me home with my neck in a plastic noose, as

I called it, and armed with painkillers. Shane opened the door and helped Nigel as best he could, showing concern and making cups of tea. Luckily Lee was in bed, so he couldn't see me in such a state.

I was sick and tired of all the troubles that life had brought with it and I must admit that I began to feel slightly sorry for myself. I had no energy left and I wanted to sleep or weep for a year, I couldn't decide which.

I did as the doctor had told me, resting as much as I could and trying to keep my neck still so as not to worsen my condition. I couldn't work, which meant that Nigel had to keep the business running on his own, pay the bills and keep a roof over our heads.

Money was tight and there was little room in the house, and I could tell Nigel was having a difficult time coping, although he never aired his worries and tried to maintain a strong front for the others and me. Yet before we knew it, another member of the family was coming to join us – Chris. Nigel's ex wife couldn't cope with her son's teenage exploits and drug experimentation, so he'd decided to live with his dad. This meant we now had three teenagers, an eight-year-old and a woman with a bad neck, all living in a three-bedroom house. It really was a nightmare and Nigel began to buckle under the tension; he started having severe heart pains. He was only forty-four and I was terrified that I'd lose him.

Harsh as it may seem, it was obvious that the older kids had to go. Nigel and I needed respite to sort our health out, and we had to concentrate on bringing in money to pay off all the debt we'd accumulated. Shane and the others were fine and completely understood the situation, finding places to stay.

Nigel's health improved and the heart pains eventually ceased, but my neck pain was intolerable and most of the time I had to dose myself up to the eyeballs on painkillers. I had no appetite and my weight plummeted, leaving me at less than eight and a half stone. The business was still shaky and Nigel and I were doing our utmost to keep everything afloat, so my stress levels were at breaking point. There were many times when I'd just curl up in a ball on my bed and cry until I simply couldn't find any tears left to shed.

Not all our news was bad, however: after three months of laser treatment I was informed that any trace of cancer had gone. The relief that swept though me was unbelievable and Nigel hugged me about a hundred times. I cried with happiness and Nigel shed a tear or two as well.

'I told you I wasn't going to die, Nigel,' I sniffed.

With my neck injury making work impossible, our insurance company found a lawyer to deal with my compensation claim from the blue chip company that had hired the driver of the van who caused the crash.

We were also hauled into court by Tom's legal representatives and grilled about the future welfare of Lee and his treatment at the hands of his dad, who was by now completely and utterly unreasonable and determined to get custody. Not for one moment was I going to let that happen, and I was relieved when, during one of the hearings, Tom's girlfriend, who was tiny and looked about twenty, was asked if Tom had ever been violent to her.

She glanced down at her hands and frowned, stumbled over her words a little, answering, 'Well, he did try to strangle me once when he lost his temper, which frightened me, but he wasn't always like that.'

I saw myself in that girl and was dying to tell her to get the hell out now, only I knew I had to keep away from my ex and that it was up to her to make her own decisions. All I could do was concentrate on Lee's situation.

Yet again, Tom was treated like he had a simple problem controlling his temper and was offered an anger management course. He refused, claiming that he didn't have a problem and that it was everyone else's fault. He thought the world and everyone in it was his enemy, and that I was his biggest adversary. The fight over our son had only just begun.

Chapter Twenty-one

Tom stared at me as I entered the court with Nigel by my side, ready to tell the judge that Lee was safe with me and that Tom wasn't a fit father.

Again, I told the judge about Tom's violence towards me and that he'd been the same with his girlfriend. Nigel voiced his views as well, standing up and stating that 'Tom is a wife-beater and has been violent towards his own son.' The judge ordered Nigel to be quiet, but Nigel wasn't about to be cowed and carried on trying to make the judge see our side.

'Lee isn't safe in the hands of this man. He should be allowed to be with his mother, where he belongs!'

The judge overruled Nigel, bellowing, 'You are in contempt of court, Sir!'

After much arguing from both sides, the judge ordered that Tom would be allowed to see Lee, only if Nigel was out of the house when he visited. Tom's face glowed with happiness and he raised an eyebrow at me. I felt like rushing over and wiping that smug smile off his face with a slap, and Nigel felt the same.

We left the hearing stunned and angry. Nigel had tried to do his best and couldn't believe that someone like Tom could spend time with Lee and he had to leave his own house.

The court order hadn't ruled that no one could be with me when Tom visited Lee at the house, so I made sure Todd was there to back me up. He was just as worried as the rest of us and, being a good friend, wasn't about to let Tom hurt

Lee again.

But we weren't vigilant enough: Tom came around to spend time with Lee, I let them out into the garden together to play cricket and the next thing I knew Lee was racing into the house, crying, 'Mum, I want Daddy to go, he keeps swearing at me because I won't go on a cricket tour with him this year.'

I told Lee to stay inside and went to face Tom, who was red in the face and had his hands on his hips. I'd had enough of his bullying and my anger overtook my fear of him. I told him to leave.

'Lee's nothing but a fucking spoilt brat!' Tom was stabbing a finger at me. 'You've turned him against me and it won't work. I'll fucking have you!'

He raised his hand to hit me and I stood my ground, replying, 'Go on then, you weak bastard, hit me and we'll see how far you get *this* time. Go on!'

At that moment Todd came up behind me and we both stared at Tom, daring him to make a move. Tom dropped his fist, looked at me, turned to Todd, then left.

'Thanks, Todd,' I said and we went back into the house, where I reassured Lee that his dad wouldn't hurt him and that everything was going to be alright.

I phoned our social worker, telling her what had happened, and she came around as soon as she could, which I was grateful for, considering that most of the ones I'd dealt with before hadn't bothered to listen to a word I said, let alone make house calls. I ranted about how stupid and irresponsible the situation was and that no one seemed to have any common sense anymore.

'What if Todd hadn't been here?' I said. 'Tom could've beaten Lee and me to a pulp! It's outrageous!'

The social worker left after reassuring me that she'd do all she could to sort the problem out and I crossed my fingers, hoping that she'd keep her word.

On and on the questions went, with Tom continuing to lie about his abuse of Lee and accusing me of being an unfit mother. My neck was very painful and our finances were in a terrible state, but I tried as best I could to stay sane. There were many times when I really thought I was going to break down and simply give up.

Chris then announced that he needed to move back in with us because his mother couldn't cope with his behaviour and his rude attitude towards her. He'd been taking drugs, getting drunk, hanging out with a bad crowd and staying out until all hours of the night. Nigel's ex was at the end of her tether, and although I'd been annoyed with her over the maintenance situation, I did feel sorry for her. Chris was a real handful. She didn't give up on her son and tried to help as best she could, agreeing with Nigel and me when we had stern words with him.

Eventually Chris left, only to be replaced by Shane and his girlfriend. They'd been on a cycling holiday in France and had run out of money and asked us to wire them enough funds to get back to the UK.

Nigel and I were up to our necks in debt and living off credit cards, so it wasn't easy to scrape the money together, but we managed it and Shane and his girlfriend moved in.

I really began to feel sorry for Nigel and, one day, while

all this was going on, I took a good look at him. He was struggling up the stairs with boxes of office equipment, and I noticed that the thick, dark hair and the twinkle in his piercing blue eyes that I'd always loved so much were gone. His hair was turning grey and his eyes were lifeless with bags underneath them. The poor man seemed to have aged overnight and I felt like crying for him.

Luckily some of the pressure was soon taken away when Shane and his girlfriend found a place to live, and I concentrated on making sure that Lee was safe and tried to keep Tom at arm's length as much as I could.

It was summertime and Nigel said, 'Great, we can sit back and relax in the garden now.'

He spoke too soon: yet another disaster was around the corner and we were facing another court case. My mortgage company wrote to tell us that I was in arrears on my flat, which I was still letting. I knew this wasn't true and guessed that there had been a mix up with the paperwork when I'd moved my mortgage from endowment to repayment. Instead of sunbathing in the garden, Nigel and I spent our evenings shuffling through mounds of files and papers trying to work out what had happened.

Josie and Todd came around to help us and they set up spreadsheets on their computer, and with Nigel playing detective we had enough evidence to prove that no money was outstanding. But my mortgage company didn't believe us, so off we went to court.

My mortgage company didn't turn up for one of the many court dates, which annoyed the judge, a kind-looking man who took my side straightaway. He read the evidence before him and not only did he rule that I owed no money, he also accused my mortgage company of wasting valuable court time and ordered them to pay all the costs that had mounted up.

I felt like kissing the judge and had tears of relief streaming down my face as Nigel and I made our way home. We could have lost our home and our business. I thanked Josie and Todd for their invaluable help, realising how blessed I was to have such friends.

That night Nigel and I got pleasantly plastered on cheap wine in our lovely garden, sharing our hopes for a brighter future – one in which Lee would live with us on a permanent basis. We had to keep positive and stay strong.

We clinked glasses, lay back in our chairs and watched as the sun went down, when all of a sudden my chair gave way and I landed with a thump on the ground and both of us shrieked with laughter.

Chapter Twenty-two

The final court hearing concerning Lee was fast approaching and I was living on my nerves. Nigel and weren't sleeping well and I was so desperate for answers that I'd been constantly praying for a sign; something that would tell me that I was going to be granted custody. My prayers were eventually answered in several different ways.

I had felt a presence in the house many times and noticed the smell of fish. The odour got stronger and stronger, until I could stand it no longer and had all the carpets cleaned. But it seemed to do no good because Nigel complained about the smell too and when Shane had been living with us he'd also moaned 'What's that awful stink, Mum?'

Around the same time, Shane had come rushing down the stairs, out of breath. I asked him what on earth was the matter and he'd replied that the mouse on his computer was moving about on its own and his computer itself was acting weirdly. Shane was a little nervous about going back into his room, especially when the fish smell got stronger.

One day, Nigel was chopping vegetables in the kitchen when an ice-cold breeze went straight through him and he said he felt a presence. I was amused, being quite used to such occurrences, and was positive that someone was trying to send me a signal or message.

I shrugged and went into the lounge, when Lee came in and asked, 'Why is Grampy standing, smiling at me in the kitchen?'

It was then that I realised I'd truly received my sign and

my stomach flipped. 'Grampy' was Tom's father, whom Lee had been very close to. He'd been dead for two years. Grampy had come to tell us that everything was going to be fine. After having a reassuring chat with Lee I felt an inner calm take over me. I was ready to face my day in court.

That day soon arrived and I put on my best suit, did my face and hair and tried to look immaculate and professional. I'd decided to represent myself because I wasn't going to trust a lawyer to fight for my son. I knew what was best for Lee and I was going to do whatever it took to win.

Tom had already sacked a couple of barristers and had hired yet another fancy lawyer to fight his case. I was quite aware I was in for a rough ride, but I crossed my fingers that the judge would side with me.

Tom was in the courtroom as I entered and threw me the most filthy look, muttering swear words. I ignored him and found my seat.

He was called to the witness box first, all decked out in a new suit and with his hair neat and slick. He didn't need much prompting to talk about how worthless I was, saying I was a lousy mother and that I had just run off, dumping Lee with him. He accused me of terrible neglect and of being an adulteress, among many other untruths.

I wanted to stand up and yell 'You lying bastard!' but it would have done no good. I had to be cool, calm and collected. Name-calling and personal jibes wouldn't win me points as far as the judge was concerned, and certainly wouldn't win me the case.

Next it was my turn to question Tom, who scowled at me from the stand.

'Why wouldn't you let us come and collect Lee's clothes and toys, when you were ordered to do so by a judge?'

'Lee's things belong where Lee belongs. With me,' he answered.

'And why have you never contributed financially to Lee's upkeep – never paid maintenance?'

'You never paid maintenance when I had Lee, so why should I?'

'Because I wasn't earning at that time and you make a lot of money.'

'That's your problem.' Tom shrugged and folded his arms.

I threw more questions his way, desperately trying to outwit him and show him up for the liar he was. I think I did a fairly good job and was relieved that my nerves hadn't shown too much.

We broke for lunch and went to the court's canteen, where I sat with Nigel practically in silence, as we were forbidden to discuss the case until it was over. Nigel threw me encouraging glances and clutched my hand across the table.

After lunch it was my turn in the witness box and I could hear Tom muttering swear words, while his lips thinned in anger. I couldn't concentrate on what was going on around me, so I asked the judge to tell Tom to stop trying to intimidate me. Tom did as he was ordered, but he stared at me with utter hate and I could see that his breathing was heavy. I was positive that if he could have he'd have jumped onto the stand and throttled me with his bare hands.

Tom's lawyer was quite gentle with me and didn't grill

me as I thought he might. I think it was obvious to him that Tom was a man with a temper and that a little boy of eight was better off with his mum.

Then the judge spoke up. 'Mrs Frampton, how would you feel if I was to give custody to your ex husband, Mr Reynolds?'

'It'll be on your conscience if you did that and I'll find a way of getting Lee back, whatever it takes,' I replied, standing straight and looking the judge right in the eyes.

Then my social worker cut in. 'As you can see, Mrs Frampton is very determined in her approach.'

'Of course I'm bloody determined! He's my son!' I wanted to shout.

The judge announced that we should all take another break while he made his decision and I sat in my seat at the back of the courtroom, clutching a locket my nan had given me. I always held it in times of stress and I needed all the reassurance I could get. I was mentally and physically exhausted and hadn't been able to eat a morsel for days, so I was light-headed and shaky.

The judge came back and addressed Tom first. I can't remember what he said, but the judge turned to me and asked me if I was aware how the custody fight had affected Lee, suggesting that perhaps I was too open and honest with my son. I couldn't understand what he was getting at and thought that I'd lost the case. The room began to swim and I was sure I was going to faint. I clutched at my chair to keep my balance.

Just as I thought I was going to lose control, the judge said the most magical words I'd heard in my life: 'Full custody is awarded to Mrs Cheryl Frampton.' I gasped, my hand flew to my mouth and tears flooded my eyes.

I thanked the judge, who answered that Lee should only see his father if he asked to and must not be forced to under any circumstances.

Tom stormed from the courtroom muttering under his breath again, but I didn't care about his threats and insults. My son was going home with Nigel and me, where he'd be safe.

I walked out into the corridor to find Nigel and when he saw the look on my face he thought we'd lost. I was so exhausted from the whole ordeal I didn't have the energy to smile or show relief. When I gave Nigel the good news he squeezed me tightly.

'I knew you'd do it,' he said.

Once we were home, I told Lee and Shane the outcome of the case and Lee cried in my arms, so pleased he wouldn't have to live with his dad again. I repeated that I loved him very much and that he'd always be safe with us.

Nigel opened a bottle of expensive wine he'd been saving for the occasion, we toasted our success and then I went to the phone to ring Dan, who I'd kept in touch with over the years, since he'd helped me gain custody of Shane. I gave Dan the whole story and voiced my surprise that the judge had seemed to concentrate on talking about me. Dan replied that because I hadn't been accusatory towards Tom and had only told the simple truth it meant the judge had warmed to me rather than take Tom's side. It also meant that it would be unlikely that my ex would be allowed to appeal.

'Thank God I had that judge,' I said to Dan. I'd often

doubted the legal system, but my faith had been restored a little.

The next day our social worker came around with a court order, stating that Tom had to stay away from Lee until he felt happy about seeing his dad again.

When the social worker had gone Lee said, 'I don't want to see Dad.'

'It's your choice now,' I replied.

Nigel, Shane, Lee and I were very close during this period of upheaval and were all looking forward to a peaceful, family Christmas. Nigel and I were still building the business up, though my neck prevented me from doing much, but we thanked our blessings for being back together.

Grampy came to visit now and again and Lee was pleased to see him, as he'd missed him when he'd died.

Lee had been attending a private school chosen by Tom, and he was just settling in there again when we received a phone call from the headmistress telling us that Tom had stopped paying the fees some time back.

Nigel and I were at a loss as to what to do; we had thousands of pounds worth of court costs to pay and very little money coming in. We knew it was going to take us years to cover our debts and we were so worried. How could we pay Lee's fees too?

But Lee's headmistress was a kind lady who really loved her job and the children in her care, and she let Lee stay on free of charge. It wasn't until a long time afterwards that we found out that she'd paid the fees from her own pocket, and although we offered to reimburse her, she wouldn't accept a penny. Nigel and I were so grateful to that lady and were sad when she died fairly recently. We will always remember her with great affection.

Unfortunately we had so much to deal with that we had to close the support group for fathers affected by the CSA. We hadn't been able to gain any support from local politicians and after arranging endless meetings and spending hours on the phone we had to give up. It was sad because there were so many harrowing stories from men whose whole lives had collapsed, leaving them broke and homeless, only we had to concentrate on keeping our own heads above water and our debts were enormous.

Work was coming in and our business was building very slowly, and then, at last, we had some good news: Nigel managed to land a fairly lucrative contract that meant we were able to pay off a few of our debts and plan a good Christmas, with presents for our kids and a big tree, decorated with bright lights and baubles. I went mad, covering our house with tinsel, holly and all kinds of hangings that sparkled. With the Victorian fireplace lit with candles and the smell of frankincense filling every room, the house was a magical place for me and I wanted it to be the best Christmas ever.

Jo came to spend the holiday period with us and I was happy to watch Nigel spend time with his daughter. She was a typical moody teenager and I still wasn't her favourite person, but I wanted Nigel and her to maintain a close bond.

Mum was staying with us too, and on Christmas morning we all got up and went downstairs to the kitchen to tuck into a big breakfast. I put a CD of carols on the stereo, and then we all went into the dining room, where I'd lit a crackling fire. Lee stopped and stared up at me; his eyes were like beacons.

'Mum, is that for me?' He was pointing at a gleaming new racing bike tied with a red bow.

I nodded and he let out a shriek of delight as he ran and climbed onto the saddle. I hadn't seen him smile so widely in a long time and all of us started to cry, seeing this little boy so happy and carefree. I wish I'd had a camera so I could keep that moment forever.

Later that day Auntie and Uncle arrived, which made me a bit nervous because it had been more than twenty years since they last spent time with my mother and I wasn't sure how they'd react towards her, after the trouble she'd caused in the past. I needn't have worried, because everyone made a special effort to get on and the celebrations went with a swing.

Shane came around with his girlfriend and her grandmother, and soon Chris joined us too. We had a full house and I was kept busy doling out food and drinks, but it was a wonderful day, filled with much laughter.

Even Tom turning up unannounced with a present for Lee didn't spoil the day, though he knew full well that he wasn't allowed to come round without Lee's permission. All the family were in the house so Lee agreed to spend a few minutes with his dad and Tom behaved himself for once.

Nighttime came and after so much excitement Auntie took ill, saying she felt faint. She'd turned a very strange colour, so I called the doctor, who gave her some pills and by Boxing Day she was healthy again.

The festivities carried on, and on New Year's Eve we threw a party for family and the close friends who'd been so good to us. We jigged all over the house to Irish music, danced to Zorba the Greek and pranced about in the garden. Midnight was soon upon us and Nigel and I hugged, saying nothing. We didn't have to; we knew what the other was thinking. We were glad to see the back of 1994.

Chapter Twenty-three

Nigel and I loved our house, as did Lee, but we decided it was time to buy our own place, so I set about visiting estate agents. Many of the houses I were shown were way out of our price range or I simply didn't like them, not until I was handed a picture of a beautiful, ivy-covered cottage, set in its own grounds with daffodils filling the garden. It was far too expensive for us, but I took the details home anyway, hoping I could concoct some plan that might enable us to buy it.

I didn't see the point in mentioning anything to Nigel because it was my little dream, and unless we came into some money or landed a lucrative contract then I couldn't see a way of us affording it. I tucked the picture into a file when I got home, but I'd take it out and have a quick peek when no one else was around.

One evening soon after, Nigel suggested that we look for a property that was big enough to house an office in, so that we could run our business from home.

'That's funny,' I said, trying to suppress my giggles. 'I think I might have found just the place.' And out came the picture of the cottage.

Nigel smiled and shook his head at me as I told him that I'd been hiding the details for days, hoping that we'd be able to buy it.

We arranged to go and see the cottage and both fell in love with it at once. The place was so charming with crooked walls and quaint windows. Nigel was particularly keen on the garden. I knew he was picturing himself reclining in his chair of an evening, a glass of wine in his hand, the birds singing in the background.

We put in an offer and it was accepted. It was a little out of our league as far as price went, but the business wasn't doing too badly and I hoped that my neck would soon get better so I could work more often and take some of the stress off Nigel.

We felt that we were really getting on with our lives and that, after the divorces and the court cases that had almost bankrupted us, we'd survived and achieved something; that we were on the up.

During the times when my neck pain was at its worst I'd think about our cottage and imagine how I'd decorate it and how happy Nigel, Lee and I were going to be when we settled there. It helped alleviate my discomfort.

Weeks before we'd booked a holiday in Disney World in Florida. I'd been worried about the amount of stress Nigel had been under and wanted him to get some rest, and I certainly needed a break. As far as finances went it probably wasn't the best idea in the world, but I told myself that I'd worry about it later.

When we'd asked Nigel's daughter Jo if she'd like to come along she hadn't shown a great deal of enthusiasm, which had disappointed Nigel. At sixteen he'd hoped she'd be excited about visiting America and such a world-famous attraction.

We did have a lovely holiday, taking in the sights and going on the rides in Disney Land, and Lee was in his element, dashing here and there and pointing at all the characters he'd seen on the TV.

'Look, Mum.' He tugged my sleeve. 'It's Goofy.'

Jo didn't enter into the holiday spirit at first, wanting to talk to her dad about her parent's divorce and why they'd split up. She still hadn't come to terms with the fact that Nigel didn't want to be with his ex wife anymore and Jo refused to accept the situation as permanent. Nigel did his best to explain to his daughter; that her mother and he had simply drifted apart. Eventually Jo seemed to understand a little of what Nigel was saying. She wasn't overly friendly with me, but the atmosphere became less tense and the four of us had some great days out, and many photos were taken to remind us of our holiday. We all returned home tanned and refreshed and Lee's case was crammed with Mickey Mouse hats and plastic Disney figures.

Moving in day arrived, which wasn't a lengthy process because we didn't have any furniture to fill it, having been living in rented accommodation, so we placed garden chairs in the sitting room and made do with whatever else we had. Nigel and I didn't care and were just happy to be in our own home. We kissed and then decided to name it 'Lover's Cottage'.

Lee adored the place and was thrilled with his new room, and couldn't prise his eyes off the garden. I knew he was itching to get out there on his racing bike and flatten the daffodils. As I predicted, Nigel was in his element in the garden too, reclining amongst the flowers and trees after a long day in our new office that we'd set up in one of the bedrooms.

I tried to make the place look as nice as possible, and we bought new furniture, but the pain in my neck was growing intolerable and I was frustrated that I could do little around the home and was only good for typing letters and filing, as far as helping Nigel went. In fact, the pain was so bad by now that I also had shooting pains down my arm, restricting movement even more. I visited the doctor and the hospital, but they were little use and just kept prescribing me pills. I had the usual physiotherapy treatment, which had no effect and also tried acupuncture and osteopathy, a success only in the short-term.

The compensation case against the blue chip company was still going ahead and my lawyer informed me that I had insurance cover of up to £50,000 to fight my cause, though I probably wouldn't need that amount.

I had to give statement after statement, repeating that I was in terrible pain and that I found it difficult to carry out everyday tasks and was unable to earn a living. I was examined and prodded by so many doctors that I thought I might as well move in to the local hospital. The doctors asked me some very peculiar questions and were far more interested in my past than the accident, and I was questioned about my sex life as well.

As Nigel drove me home after untold check-ups I'd seethe, 'I'm sick of quacks!'

Nigel always managed to calm me down and when we got home he'd sit me in the garden and place a welcome glass of wine in my hand.

I began to feel depressed and the constant questions and

the inability to do much to help Nigel with the business were affecting my confidence. I'm ashamed to admit it, but occasionally I felt jealous of him for being out and about meeting people. I missed the interaction that being employed brought with it and sometimes caught myself indulging in self-pity. That didn't last for long because I knew how hard Nigel was working and had to cope with everything alone, plus the bills were mounting at an alarming rate.

The feeling of being useless and the nagging pain often drove me to tears, although I did try to hide my emotions from my family. Lee looked up at me one day and touched my hand, asking me what was wrong. I told him that I'd be fine and that I was just sad because my neck hurt.

Soon I had to have a stern word with myself: 'Stop moaning and sitting on your backside, Cheryl. Do something, woman.'

There wasn't much I could do to assist Nigel, but I was able to write music and sing - talents that didn't take much movement. I thought perhaps I might bring in some earnings if I sold a song.

I asked Shane if he'd be interested in composing a melody to match my lyrics and he agreed. He was, and still is, a talented musician and I was pleased to be able to work on a project with my son. Shane had the equipment we needed, so along with another songwriter friend of mine, John, who'd enjoyed success in the eighties, we began working on some songs.

John and I spent hours on the lyrics and vocals (John played the guitar too) and Shane concentrated on the music.

There were a few disagreements and tantrums at first, until we eventually settled down and all animosity was forgotten. We made a good team.

We hired a local recording studio, which was owned by a really nice guy Ian, who'd worked with many famous artists, so we felt quite privileged to be there. The owner was a great source of help and encouragement to Shane and was terrific on the production side of the recording, and he, Shane and I struck up an immediate friendship.

It wasn't until we had recorded another two songs that we got our first publishing deal with a fairly well known company, and the three of us couldn't believe our good fortune when another deal followed suit. I even forgot my neck pain for a while - I was so overjoyed that I finally had musical success after all those years of struggling and being told I was 'no spring chicken.'

There was more good news to follow when 'Passion' got signed to an American publisher. That really was a great day for me, considering that I'd trudged around British record companies desperately trying to market it. Someone actually appreciated my talent. How I wished I could have called Cowell and all those executives who sat behind their shiny desks and told me I was an over-the-hill flop.

Nigel was so pleased for me and I must admit I couldn't help but enjoy a bit of a crow about my good fortune. 'Ha! Look at all those people who said I couldn't be a success in the precious music business. Well, stuff them all!'

My case against the blue chip company was hotting up too: it turned out that while I was out shopping with Shane and his girlfriend one day, they'd secretly filmed me to see if I was mobile. I'd explained a hundred times that it wasn't my legs that were affected, just moving my neck and arm was a problem, and that I was unable to work. How many more times did I have to justify myself to these people? How many more times were they going to make out that I was intent on conning money out of them under false pretences?

As if I wasn't livid enough, I also found out that they'd edited the tape to make me look as if I was some kind of nubile athlete.

'Right!' I raged to Nigel. 'If they want a fight they've got one!'

My lawyer was furious too and he proved that parts of the tape where I was rubbing my neck or stopping to take a rest had been edited. The company came forward and offered me a small amount of money as compensation, but on the advice of my lawyer, I turned the pitiful offer down and prepared to go to court once again. If I'd known about the dirty tricks that would be played and that the case would drag on for two years, I'm not so sure that I'd have made that decision. I'd had enough of court battles.

I realised that I had no choice but to fight back, because soon I began to suspect that our phone was being tapped. Sometimes there was a funny crackling on the line and it sounded as if someone was picking up on another extension. I decided to contact a security company for advice. They told me that my phone could well have been tampered with and a company such as the one I was dealing with were more than capable of doing so.

It wasn't long before I realised that I was being followed too. When out shopping I was constantly glancing behind me or ducking into shop doorways. Passers-by must have thought I'd been released from the local psychiatric hospital. It reminded me of the days I'd had to hide from Luke by wearing a disguise, and I even considered buying a wig and large hat. Nigel said that that was just silly.

I grew terribly paranoid, wondering where this person was going to pop up, and although I hardly ever managed to get a proper glimpse of him I could feel his presence behind me whenever I left the house. I found out later on that my 'stalker' had even carried a camera.

'It's going to be alright, babe,' said Nigel. 'You'll see.'

But I wasn't quite so sure any more. My hope and the positive side of my nature that had got me through so many hard times were beginning to dwindle. I was so very tired.

The morning of my first day in court I thought I was going to be physically sick. I hated having to face lawyers and the endless questions and accusations again, and I felt like absconding, just disappearing somewhere far away. It wasn't an option though, so I got dressed in my smartest outfit and off Nigel and I went. On the way to court I reassured myself that three days wasn't that long and it that would all be over before I knew it.

The first day was truly awful: I stood shaking in the witness box, with my grandmother's gold locket clutched in my sweaty hand, as question after question was thrown at me. The opposition's barrister was tough and was forever interrupting what I had to say and reminding me to 'answer yes or no, Mrs Frampton. Yes or no! It's as simple as that!' He was a large middle-aged man in an expensive pin-stripe suit and you could tell that he had years of experience behind him. I knew my barrister was no match against such an imposing character, particularly as mine was in his late twenties and looked as if he'd fall over if you blew on him.

The questions came thick and fast and it was apparent that the barrister was trying to confuse me and get me to admit to something that wasn't true. I wasn't going to let that happen though; I was under oath, I was sticking to the truth and no one, not even an arrogant barrister, was going to make me look like a fool.

Then something happened to make the barrister appear rather foolish; it even had the judge smirking.

The barrister held up a photograph of my back garden, showing a lawn and a child's swing, and asked, pacing up and down the courtroom for effect: 'So, with such a *severe* neck injury, as you claim to have, how do you manage to move such a heavy object to mow the lawn, Mrs Frampton?'

'What a stupid question,' I thought. 'Why on earth would you have to move a swing to mow a lawn?' I didn't make sense. Not that I even mowed the lawn anyway. Nigel did, and we never had a swing, since Lee was eleven and too old for one.

The barrister's eyebrows rose and he folded his arms in front of him. 'Can you answer that?' he asked, chuffed at his cleverness.

I was trying terribly hard not to laugh. 'Yes, that is my back garden,' I said, 'but it's not my swing. The estate agent we bought the house through took that picture, and the swing belonged to the previous owner's children. I don't have young children, as you know, so we don't have a swing and therefore nothing to move when we mow the lawn.'

I'm sure the barrister blushed, but his bravado took over and he fired more questions at me, until the end of the first day arrived.

I was so relieved to leave that courtroom and encouraging words from Auntie and Nigel helped to bolster my confidence and give me a little hope. Although Nigel did his utmost to keep me positive and comfort me, it upset him deeply to have to stand by and watch me go through such a harrowing experience on my own. He told me he felt helpless and I knew it made him angry.

The second day came and it was my barrister's turn. He looked like a little boy in that courtroom and I remember thinking that I didn't stand a chance of winning and that no one would take him seriously. But he wasn't as bad as I'd imagined, and he managed to get the man who'd taped me to admit that it had been edited afterwards.

The third day turned out to be the worst, because I was told to bring along the diary that I'd kept since the accident. I'd been advised to do this by my legal representative. This journal contained my most intimate thoughts and details, and I had been foolish to be too open about my personal life, especially as it was to be scrutinised by the whole court.

My journal had been photocopied and, right in front of me, the copies were handed around to practically everyone in the courtroom. Angrily, I told the judge that having people read my personal diary was unacceptable and that it had no relevance to the case. He barked that I had no choice in the matter, and then I was informed that my case was to be adjourned for a month. At the end of that month I was to face yet another three-day court hearing. I couldn't believe what the judge was saying and I looked down at my Nan's locket, shaking my head slowly from side to side, tears welling in my eyes.

Chapter Twenty-four

The month leading up to my next court hearing was filled with sleepless nights and days of pacing my living room, especially as I was still under oath and wasn't allowed to discuss the proceedings with anyone, even my husband.

When the case began again I was in for several terrible shocks. The fact that the diary I'd been keeping had been passed around and scrutinised by all involved was the least of my worries - the lowest point came when I was asked to hand in Ben's suicide note. When Ben had taken his own life I'd had no idea that he'd left a letter behind because my mother had taken it and hidden it in a drawer in her house. Years later she'd admitted that she'd kept it and handed it over to me. I broke down when I read his words about how much he'd loved Shane and me and how terribly inadequate he'd felt. My hands shook as I saw the blood that smudged his words and I imagined the pain he'd gone through. The note even explained that he'd tried to hang himself once and hadn't been able to achieve even that. The coroner handling the case confirmed that Ben's first attempt that fateful evening had been botched and that's why the paper was speckled with blood. I hate to think about what the poor man must have endured.

I remember my mother's quiet voice as the whole story came out and the way she looked at me when she passed me the crumpled paper. I think she expected me to be angry and shout at her for keeping such a secret. I didn't show anger though. I was so upset by the sight of Ben's handwriting that

233

I'd been too traumatised to ask Mum why she'd left it so long to show me the note. I accepted any explanation Mum offered and concentrated on getting on with my life.

Now I was faced with prying strangers who had no concern for my feelings and I couldn't believe that anyone could be so callous or macabre – all in the name of money. What on God's earth did Ben's last words have to do with a compensation case?

'Shane,' I thought. 'What if Shane hears about this?'

I'd told Shane that his dad had left a letter behind, but he didn't feel ready to read it. He still hasn't, and it's up to him whether he takes that step or not. That's why I was furious that such a painful part of our lives was being bandied about like a cheap joke.

The blue chip company had really done its homework and as I stood in the witness stand again I was also questioned about the comments I'd made in my diary regarding my sex life and how my injury had affected it. I scolded myself for being so honest and wished I'd filled the pages with cake recipes and mundane facts.

I'd written something about losing my libido and that foreplay was almost non-existent. This was picked up by the opposition's barrister, and I was so disgruntled and humiliated about my private life being put on public display that my answer reflected my mood:

'It's like this, right. You know when a man plays with certain parts of your body; well you're supposed to feel something, *aren't* you? I don't and it's not because I don't love or want my husband. I'm in too much pain to think about anything except keeping my neck still. Got it *now*?'

The barrister was silent for a few seconds and I glared at him. I was well and truly sick of his jibes and arrogance; the way that he postured around the courtroom like he was starring in a badly directed Shakespearean drama.

Next up was the neurosurgeon who I'd visited many times about my neck; I wasn't at all happy to see him take the stand because he was just as arrogant as the opposing barrister. By now I'd realised that my legal representative was no Perry Mason and during the month I'd been waiting for my case to be taken back into the courtroom I'd nearly bitten all my nails off, I was so worried about what was going to happen.

As the neurosurgeon took his oath I twiddled my grandmother's locket so manically that I almost dropped it on the floor. My barrister stood up to begin his line of questioning and I looked at him and felt like straightening his tie and ordering him to speak louder. I noticed that his shoes were scuffed and that he had an annoying habit of scratching his head.

'Great. I've had it now,' I thought.

My barrister questioned the doctor about my injuries and I began to feel a little more confident, until he got the doctor to admit that even if my injury wasn't physically serious enough to warrant my staying off work, the psychological implications were enough to cause me to be unemployed.

I wanted to stand up and shout that I wasn't imagining my discomfort and that none of them had any idea what I'd been through. The judge then asked if the doctor would like to rephrase his answer.

'Yes, I feel as if I might have been coerced into giving the wrong answer,' he said.

The opposing barrister wasn't about to give up, and seeing that my legal representative had made a fatal mistake, broke in with several lines of questioning that completely undermined me.

My barrister sat and twiddled his pencil, looking at the ground, as the judge announced that the case was over. The representatives from the blue chip company almost hugged with joy. I'd lost. Years of physical pain and constant worry had come to nothing.

I almost fell off the witness stand and had to hold on to a chair for support. The room circled and the dizziness made me nauseous.

My solicitor informed me that my insurance would cover the court costs and that I was to be given a thousand pounds by the blue chip company as a kind of goodwill gesture.

'Shove it!' I wanted to shriek at those corporate sharks with their pinstriped suits and smug faces, but I was just too tired to get angry or show anyone how completely desolate I felt. It was over and I wanted to go home. I wanted to get out of that stuffy courtroom and never, ever go back. I wanted to be with my husband, my kids and my dog.

Nigel took my hand and led me to the car, huffing and puffing, his arm waving in the air. 'Who the hell do these people think they are? Bloody swines!' Unlike me, Nigel never swore, so that was pretty strong language for him.

I couldn't think anymore, let alone answer. I'd given it my best shot and lost. That was that. I just felt like going to sleep and when we got home that's exactly what I did, for days.

FOR CRYING OUT LOUD

Christmas 1997 came and went and it was a cold January morning when I came in from walking the dog to find a letter on the doormat. I recognised my lawyer's envelope and shouted to Nigel that our money had come. I knew it was a pittance, but I thought we could use the cash to pay off some of our credit card bills.

Nigel was at my side as I opened the letter and we both almost collapsed on the floor when we saw its contents: a bill for £36,000. Our legal representative had gone well over the limit set by my insurance company and hadn't thought to tell Nigel and I about the mounting costs.

My hand shook and the letter slipped out of my grasp. 'Nigel...' I couldn't finish my sentence; I couldn't even cry. My husband was silent too, and his expression told me he was as numb as I.

We decided to take our time and wait for further news from our lawyer and shortly afterwards we were sent another letter. With sickening dread I opened it to find that, indeed, a mistake had been made and that the first bill had been revised. The second letter stated that we actually owed £42,000. It transpired that my lawyer had used my case to further his career and kept information about the mounting costs from me, hoping that we'd win and he'd be seen as a young hotshot. Only he hadn't been a match for his courtroom opponent. Now Nigel and I were to pay for his mistakes. I felt like strangling the man with my bare hands.

'What a moron! I shouted, sending the dog hiding behind the sofa. 'What the hell was he thinking?'

'He wasn't thinking.' Nigel's head shook from side to side. 'The man's a joke.'

'And not a funny one! I'm going around his office to fucking thump him!'

Nigel put his hand on my shoulder. 'Cheryl, we've seen enough of courtrooms.' My wise husband was always right.

Nigel and I tried to carry on as best we could in the circumstances, he running the business and me looking after Lee and the house. I still typed the odd letter and helped out with filing and phone calls, but my neck and arm pain was a hindrance.

We talked at length about where we were going to get the money to cover the costs of the case and were relieved when a phone call from Nigel's ex left us with what we thought was a solution.

True to her word from years before, she said that she was going to sell their house as part of their divorce settlement and he was to receive half of the proceeds. We were both surprised at this news, not really believing that she'd stick to her word, but it seemed she'd remembered her pledge and was going to do the right thing by Nigel, which meant he was owed thousands. I was very impressed, as she didn't have to give us a penny - the house being in her name solely - and we both thanked her. It meant we could pay the court fees and get ourselves out of debt. We almost danced with relief.

Our relief didn't last long though, as Nigel's ex said he was to give equal amounts of money to Jo and Chris out of his half, which would leave him with a small portion. Of course, Nigel didn't want to see his kids go without, but he thought Jo, at eighteen, was too young for such a large amount of money. She'd also informed him that she wanted to buy a house with her boyfriend, which alarmed Nigel all the more.

'What if they split up? He could get half of her house,' Nigel said to me one evening.

Chris was older and had grown into a sensible young man, and decided that he was going to invest his windfall, which pleased Nigel.

I was furious and thought that Nigel's ex should have handed Nigel his half of the proceeds of the house and left it to him to decide what to do with it. Not once since their divorce had Nigel neglected Jo and Chris emotionally or financially and I felt she was trying to get back at him in some way. Perhaps she thought that if something happened to Nigel his money would be left to me and I'd pass it on to my own children.

I hated to see my husband so downhearted, and his mood was made worse by the fact that Jo wouldn't listen to his reasoning and sent him a rude letter, bringing up the past and blaming him for her parents' marriage break-up.

Nigel wanted to let matters lie, but I wasn't about to let a stroppy eighteen-year-old hurt my husband so deeply and I wrote Jo a strong letter in reply, which didn't go down very well.

We then went to a solicitor to receive advice about the whole house and money situation, which turned out to be the best action we'd taken in a long time because we also mentioned what had happened with the blue chip company and our resulting debts. The solicitor was a lovely man and was genuinely appalled by our story. He promised to look in to the case and asked us to give him all the relevant paperwork. Nigel and I left his office feeling less despondent.

True to his word, our solicitor, along with his hard-working assistant, pored over the piles of photocopied paperwork we'd given them and soon I found myself making lengthy statements and reading letters from the blue chip company and their legal representatives. Talk about going around in circles.

'I can't face court, Nigel. Whatever happens, I can't face another courtroom,' I groaned.

'It'll be okay, babe.' Nigel smiled.

Life had to carry on and Nigel concentrated on the business, while I wrote song lyrics and practised my singing. Shane was doing well with his music too and Lee was happy at school and spending the evenings with his friends or racing around on his bike.

I hoped that our solicitor would dig up something that meant we wouldn't have to pay such heavy costs and I spoke to Auntie and my mum about the situation as well. They were both encouraging and Mum said that I should wait, that it would all come out in my favour in the end.

Mum also had a rather interesting proposition for me: her relationship with Lucy seemed to be going well and she was keen for me to meet and make up with my sister. I was nervous about seeing Lucy again and wondered if she'd forgive me for telling the family about Rebecca's parentage. It had turned out that, according to medical evidence, there was little doubt that Robert actually was Rebecca's real dad, and he'd forgiven Lucy for her affair with his friend all those years ago.

I was glad that I hadn't broken up her family with my interference and said to Mum that if Lucy was happy to see me then I'd love to catch up with her.

Lucy sent me a letter stating her point-of-view, and although I didn't agree with everything she said I could tell she was very keen to have me back in her life, so I wrote to her, giving my side of the story and replying that I hoped we could make up.

Not long afterwards Lucy phoned and we arranged for her to visit a few weeks later. The morning of our reunion my stomach was churning, I was so afraid that we'd argue, but I needn't have worried because as soon as I opened my front door we rushed into each other's arms and cried.

'I've missed you, love,' Lucy said, tears trickling over her cheeks.

'I missed you too.' I gave my sister another big cuddle.

Not wanting to leave Sheena out of the celebrations, I rang her and we all got together. We talked about the past, our mother and all our differences over the years and made a pact that we wouldn't give up on one another again. We agreed that sisters should stick together and that, in the future, we'd talk rather than fall out.

Mum was less than impressed. She was pleased that I was talking to Lucy, yet she hated the fact that Sheena was involved in our reunion. Mum and Sheena hadn't spoken for years and I knew then, as I know now, that they never would. Both were, and are, stubborn women. I can't blame Sheena for her attitude towards our mother. God only knows how many problems I'd had with Mum, but Sheena really did bear the brunt of our mum's temper and cruel words.

Sheena will never forgive Mum for her past actions and I still hold on to the hope that my sister will try to let go of her hurt and anger. I wish that her days could be more carefree and I hope that when she reads this book she'll let some of her pain go and remember that she does have people around her who love her and that life is lighter and easier if you don't harbour bitterness. She owes herself so much more.

Nigel came into the living room one morning and announced that we only had enough money to pay two months' mortgage, so as we'd reluctantly discussed, we put our beautiful cottage on the market and prepared to move to a cheaper property.

The house-sale seemed to take forever, but the day arrived when we had to leave our home. Nigel, Lee and I shed a tear or two, even if we knew it was for the best and that it was time to make a new start. We'd found a modern four-bedroom property in Crawley, which wasn't nearly as pretty as our old cottage but it had a large garden, and Nigel decided to convert the garage into a dining room to give us more room. The house wasn't big enough to include an office so we had to rent space nearby.

Luckily, my neck pain was diminishing by the week and with several more visits to doctors and extra acupuncture treatments I was able to involve myself in the business more.

At the time Nigel and I had been looking for a new place to live, Shane had come around and told us that he was going to buy a house on an estate in Crawley. Low and behold, it transpired that it was practically in the same road as our new home.

When I look out of my window now I can see Shane's front gate, and not long ago I said, 'You won't be able to get away with anything, Shane. I'll see all the women coming and going.'

Shane gave me a big grin: 'You always know things before I do, Mum, so what's new?'

The spiritual side of my beliefs has always been a bit of a mystery to my son, but although he won't admit it and likes to make jokes I think he actually does have a deep faith that there is another side to life and realises that his mum isn't as daft as she sometimes appears.

Within weeks of moving into our new home, Nigel and I had some news that made us realise that the bad times were behind us and we could begin again. Our solicitor had worked hard on our case and proved that we didn't owe a penny; in fact we were still to receive the £1,000 compensation we were meant to get from the blue chip company in the first place. We didn't need to appear in court and there were to be no more questions, statements or accusations. The fight was over at long last. Nigel and I threw our arms around each other and laughed until we cried.

Epilogue

When I reached the grand old age of thirty-five I felt happier than I ever had. I wasn't happy that I was thirty-five, of course, and would have liked to have been twenty-five instead, but my marriage and home life was happy and secure, as it is has continued to be since. I thank Nigel and my two lovely sons every day for that.

In 2001 Shane turned twenty-six - the same age that his father was when he had killed himself two decades before and, knowing this, my son began to ask questions about Ben. We'd talked about his dad many times since Shane was little, but he needed to know more. He decided he wanted to find out what had happened to his dad's house and belongings, as he had nothing of Ben's, only odd photos.

I spoke to my mother, once again asking what had happened to the proceeds of our house sale in Adelaide and Mum grew angry, demanding to know what I was accusing her of. I explained that Shane had unanswered questions about his father and that he was of an age where he was bound to be curious. Mum just became more and more defensive and the arguments intensified, reminding me of the past.

In the end I grew tired of the whole situation and resigned myself to the fact that Shane and I would never know exactly what my mother did concerning the house in Australia and any insurance policies. It had all happened so long ago and I'd had enough of bickering and the bad feeling that had always soured my mother's and my relationship.

I seriously began to doubt if we might be able to enjoy something that resembled a mother and daughter relationship and after countless letters and a hurtful phone call I came to the conclusion that I simply couldn't involve Mum in my life any more. It was too painful and our last conversation proved that there was no middle ground.

'Well, at least I didn't lose my kids to Social Services!' she shouted.

I couldn't be bothered to explain myself and didn't feel the need to. I 'd made my mistakes and I'd rectified them years before. My sons were grown up and secure, and her comment had no bearing on our lives any more.

'Mum, I know I've never been perfect and nor have you, but you just can't help yourself, can you? What a terrible thing to say to your own daughter. I'm sorry, Mum, I am truly, but I won't be in touch with you again. Goodbye, Mum.' I put the phone down. My emotions were a blend of sadness and relief.

Lucy continues to call me about the situation and tells me about my mother's distress, asking if I'll speak to Mum. I've answered that I'm willing to be civil and chat to her on the phone now and then, but for my own good I can't keep trying to sustain a deeper connection with her. She's my mother, so I have a respect for her and hope that she's well and happy, but I don't want to involve her in my life. Most of all, I'm sorry that my sons don't have a relationship with their grandmother.

In November 2001 I flew out to Australia after being told that my dad was in hospital, on his deathbed. The twenty-four-hour flight was excruciating and I prayed to God that I'd get to speak to Dad; that he'd make a miraculous recovery. I rushed into his ward, breathless and tearful, to find him on a life-support machine.

I stayed by his bedside for almost a month, begging him to 'hold on and not give up.' My prayers were answered and eventually he was well enough to be taken off the life-support machine. He had indeed made a truly miraculous recovery, which surprised all the medical staff who had battled to save him.

Dad's health still isn't great, but he manages to get about. I make sure that I speak to him on the phone as often as possible and I wish that Australia wasn't thousands of miles away, so I could visit him. Still, at least I know he has his wife and other family members with him.

Sadly, Auntie Joyce passed away in 2001 and I miss her each and every day. I hope that she looks down on me from above and is proud that I have put my past behind me, and also that she approves of this book. I think she would and that's one of the many reasons I've dedicated it to her. Without Auntie, I wouldn't be where I am today.

The bad relationships, the violence, the courtroom dramas are far behind me now and I recovered enough from my neck injury years ago to go back to work with Nigel on a part-time basis.

Although our business continues to fluctuate, like many do,

Nigel has a burning ambition that we hope will come to fruition in the near future. He has always been a huge music fan and spends hours scouring independent music shops for rare CDs, and he would love to open his own place, selling everything from jazz and reggae to the blues, funk and classical music. Nigel has diverse tastes and our house is literally filled with CDs by the most obscure artists that ever entered a recording studio to legendary groups such as The Beatles and ABBA.

Nigel has always stood by me and has undergone a lot of stress because of my bad choices, and I sincerely hope that he'll get his music shop. I hope that he can recline behind his counter, as he does in our garden, with a glass of red wine in his hand, listening to his favourite tracks and chatting to browsing customers. He deserves it.

Last year was our tenth wedding anniversary and we decided to reaffirm our wedding vows. But so many people wanted to be a part of the arrangements that it was fast becoming a full-blown wedding again, so we decided to sneak off to a small hotel instead.

'Never mind, love, we can do it another time,' I said. Reaffirming our vows was important to me, but I was just glad to have some time to ourselves.

We arrived at the country hotel and I was surprised to find that Nigel had arranged for our room to be filled with flowers and champagne. A beautiful four-poster bed took pride of place in the middle of the room and I thought how lucky I was to have such a romantic husband. Nigel cracked open the champagne and we wished each other a happy anniversary.

Nigel then told me that we couldn't go out to dinner until a little later, as he was waiting for a phone call.

'What phone call?' I kept asking him. 'What's going on?'

And then it happened. Unbeknown to me, Nigel had arranged for the vicar who'd originally married us to ring us so we could reaffirm our wedding vows by conference phone. He had even given the vows I'd written all those years ago to the vicar for us to repeat.

Nigel was so full of emotion that he could hardly speak and I just kept smiling at him, unable to take in the fact that he'd gone to so much trouble to make my day special. It was a moment I'll never forget and constantly reminds me that the past is so far behind me that it's almost as if it never occurred. Nigel helped make that happen and I will always love him dearly for it.

Shane's music career is going well and we have continued to write together. I'm so proud that his courage and determination have not only seen him through many difficult periods but he's now very successful in his field, writing music for movies. Recently he even went to the Cannes Film Festival on a producer's yacht. I wait patiently for the day that he becomes filthy rich so that I can retire before I reach fifty.

As for Lee, many months ago he gave me a big shock. He'd driven Nigel and me to distraction, blasting heavy rock from the stereo in his bedroom, but suddenly he became a jazz fan, and we have since been serenaded by Count Basie and other artists. This overnight change has done wonders for my nerves and I'm glad to say that Lee has turned out to be a talented musician like his brother. He plays the drums and I think that one day he'll be famous in his own right.

Nigel's kids are doing well too; Chris is a caring, sensitive young man, and he and I enjoy many in-depth chats covering all manner of subjects and I love being in his company, while Jo and I have buried our differences and get along well. We've learnt a lot from each other over the years and we recently attended her beautiful wedding in the Bahamas.

My faith and the many signs and messages I have received over the years have had a huge influence on my life, and I'm especially grateful to Ben. I know it was he who came to my aid on more than one occasion, and I have to thank my spirit guide Manu, who has been at my side for a while now. He has been a great source of inspiration.

When I think back to those dark years, I'm so happy that I found the strength to keep positive and remind myself that if I just hung on a little bit longer I'd be fine in the end. I'd like to say to anyone reading this book who is in a similar situation to the ones I found myself in – don't give in. Keep strong and remember that what you are going through now, what you experience tomorrow or the next day, won't necessarily be the same next week or next year. However hard the mental or physical blows come raining down, look into your soul and keep your hope, determination and dreams with you always. Ask for help; ask for a sign and you could well find that life will have a funny way of surprising you.

Listed below are useful contact numbers. By contacting any one of these numbers, you are taking the first step to receiving help for yourself and your children.

National Domestic Violence Helpline.
Open 365 days a year, 24 hours a day.
All calls are confidential: **0870 599 5443**

Women's Aid: **0845 702 3468**

Police: Ask for Domestic Violence Unit: **0845 607 0999**

Refuge: (24 hour Crisis Line) **0870 599 5443**

Victim Support: **0845 303 0900**

North Sussex Women's Aid: **01293 522 994**

Sussex Police: **0845 607 0999**

NSPCC: (24 hour Child Protection Line) **0800 800 500**